Curtiss Navy I

in action

By Peter Bowers
Color by Don Greer
Illustrated by Joe Sewell

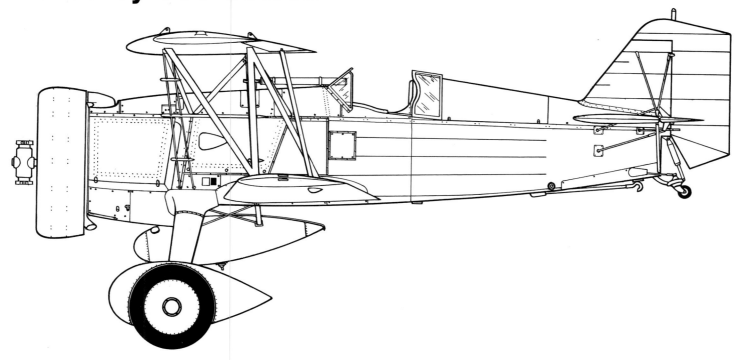

Aircraft Number 156

squadron/signal publications

This BFC-2 was assigned to VB-2B aboard USS SARATOGA (CV-3). This unit flew the Goshawk for some five years, first at the F11C-2 (VF-1B), and finally ending up as VB-3 with BFC-2s When the squadron was redesignated as VB-3, the tail color was changed to White.

Acknowledgments

Harold Andrews
F.H. Dean
F.W. Gemeinhardt
William T. Larkins
David W. Lucabaugh
Kenn C. Rust
San Diego Aerospace Museum
Stan Staples

Dedication

To Admiral William A. Moffett who, as Chief of the Bureau of Aeronautics from 1921 to 1933, did more than any other individual to promote the development of U.S. Naval Aviation, even in the face of strong opposition from the traditional "Battleship Admirals". He died at sea aboard the airship USS AKRON on the night of 3/4 April 1933.

ISBN 0-89747-342-6

If you have any photographs of aircraft, armor, soldiers or ships of any nation, particularly wartime snapshots, why not share them with us and help make Squadron/Signal's books all the more interesting and complete in the future. Any photograph sent to us will be copied and the original returned. The donor will be fully credited for any photos used. Please send them to:

Squadron/Signal Publications, Inc.
1115 Crowley Drive
Carrollton, TX 75011-5010

Если у вас есть фотографии самолётов, вооружения, солдат или кораблей любой страны, особенно, снимки времён войны, поделитесь с нами и помогите сделать новые книги издательства Эскадрон/Сигнал ещё интереснее. Мы переснимем ваши фотографии и вернём оригиналы. Имена приславших снимки будут сопровождать все опубликованные фотографии. Пожалуйста, присылайте фотографии по адресу:

Squadron/Signal Publications, Inc.
1115 Crowley Drive
Carrollton, TX 75011-5010

軍用機、装甲車両、兵士、軍艦などの写真を所持しておられる方はいらっしゃいませんか？どの国のものでも結構です。作戦中に撮影されたものが特に良いのです。Squadron/Signal社の出版する刊行物において、このような写真は内容を一層充実し、興味深くすることができます。当方にお送り頂いた写真は、複写の後お返しいたします。出版物中に写真を使用した場合は、必ず提供者のお名前を明記させて頂きます。お写真は下記にご送付ください。

Squadron/Signal Publications, Inc.
1115 Crowley Drive
Carrollton, TX 75011-5010

An F6C-3 (BuNo 7138) of the Red Rippers, VB-1B, stationed aboard USS LEXINGTON (CV-2). Until July of 1928, this unit had been a fighter squadron (VF-5), using the same aircraft and serving on the same carrier. F6C-3s stationed aboard ship had their original landing gear replaced by F6C-4 type landing gear. (Joseph Malta F. Haase via San Diego Aerospace Museum)

3

Introduction

The Curtiss Aeroplane & Motor Company was the largest aircraft manufacturer in the U.S. during the First World War, but its principal products were low-powered training aircraft and slow twin-engined flying boats. The firm had designed and built a few unarmed and unsuccessful single seat scouts, but had produced nothing that could be called a high-performance aircraft.

Curtiss' first experience with up-to-date high-performance types began late in 1917 when it received large government contracts to build established French and British aircraft. A contract to build 2,000 two-seat British Bristol F.2B fighters ended disastrously after only twenty-six were built. The government had insisted that the 250 hp British Rolls-Royce "Eagle" engine be replaced with the new 400 hp American "Liberty" engine. The Bristol was not adaptable to such a major change, and the contract was canceled after several fatal accidents. The contract for 3,000 French Spad XIII fighters was canceled before a single aircraft had been built, and only one aircraft on an order for 1,000 British S.E.5 fighters was actually delivered.

Curtiss design experience with high-performance aircraft began early in 1918, after the government abandoned its policy of having U.S. industry build foreign designs and permitted the development of purely domestic combat models. The first developed by Curtiss was the Model 18-T (original designation, Model 15 under the 1935 system) "Wasp" triplane. This was a two-seat fighter powered by the revolutionary 400 hp Curtiss-Kirkham K-12 engine and was briefly the world's fastest aircraft, with a top speed at full military load of 163 mph.

The end of the war ended development of the two Wasp prototypes, but because of their speed, the Navy used them as racers into 1923. Curtiss; however, went on to win production orders for aircraft designed by other firms under the odd government procurement policies of the time. If the Army or Navy bought a prototype aircraft from a designer/builder, it also acquired the rights to the design. If production models were wanted, the requesting service would invite bids from the entire industry. Often, some firm other than the aircraft designer won the production order.

Under this procedure, Curtiss built fifty 300 hp Orenco D fighters and fifty Martin MB-2/NBS-1 bombers, but none of these traditional designs did anything to advance the technology base at Curtiss.

Curtiss also took part in another government program. The Army Air Service Engineering Division had designed a new aircraft, the PN-1 (Pursuit, Night) and invited bids from the

The first fighters Curtiss built for the Navy were thirty-four TS-1s, designed by the Navy Bureau of Aeronautics. The aircraft were used aboard the USS LANGLEY (CV-1). (USN)

industry for the building of two prototypes. Curtiss won the contract, but it was such an unsatisfactory aircraft that only one of the two was completed and it was not flown. Curtiss got one very significant technological benefit from it; however, an introduction into welded steel tube fuselage construction techniques.

Curtiss did some highly original work in developing racing aircraft that used later versions of the K-12 engine, first as the CD-12 and later as the plain D-12. These racers used the semi-monocoque laminated wooden fuselage construction of the "Wasp" and set several world speed records, as well as winning major races from 1921 through 1925. In some Navy procurement paperwork the racers were disguised as new experimental fighters since Congress might consider racing aircraft to be unnecessary frivolities in the 1920-1924 period of postwar austerity.

Curtiss' first production order for a Navy fighter came in 1922 when it was low bidder for a contract to build thirty-four TS-1 shipboard fighters designed by the Navy's Bureau of Aeronautics (BuAer). Navy serial numbers (called Bureau Number [BuNos] because they were assigned by the Bureau of Aeronautics) were A-6248/6270 and A-6305/6315. As a check on production time and cost, the Naval Aircraft Factory in Philadelphia built five others, BuNos A-6300/6304.

Again, the low-powered (200 hp) design did nothing to advance Curtiss technology, but Curtiss won a 1924 Navy contract to redesign the wood-frame TS-1 into an all-metal aircraft. The two built (BuNos A-6689, 6690) were designated as F4C-1s in tacit recognition of the fact that the three preceding racer models for the Navy had been given F-for-Fighter designations. The designation F4C-1 translates as F (ighter), 4th fighter by C (Curtiss), -1 (initial configuration)

The next Curtiss Navy fighter, was a duplicate of the contemporary U.S. Army P-1 Hawk fighter, built under the designation F6C-1. The logical F5C designation was skipped deliberately because there were a large number of wartime F-5L flying boats still in service and it was thought that two F-5 models in service simultaneously would be confusing. Despite the claims of a well-known aviation artist/historian, there was no Navy equivalent of the Army Curtiss PW-8 designated the F5C.

Navy Curtiss Hawks

Starting with the F6C-1 Hawk in 1925, Curtiss single-seat fighters for the Navy continued through 1934 with the F7C-1 Seahawk, the F9C Sparrowhawk, and the F11C/BFC Goshawk. It should be pointed out; however, that none of these names were official. Curtiss had given bird names to most of its aircraft models since 1919. Even though the armed forces did not use names for their aircraft, Curtiss applied them to its military models in advertising and other publicity. The name, "Hawk" was pushed very hard and figured heavily in Curtiss' considerable export sales of those designs.

Aircraft Costs

The unit cost of military aircraft varies greatly depending on the circumstances of the sale. A single prototype costs much more than a quantity production model since much of the builder's development cost is charged to that one unit. In production quantities, unit costs are greatly reduced because development costs have usually been written off against the prototype, hard tooling costs for the production models can be amortized over many units, and raw materials and equipment costs per unit are greatly reduced through a volume purchase.

For military aircraft , the unit costs are the price paid to the builder for the completed airframe. Most of the equipment, power plant, armament, instruments, electronics, and sometimes even wheels and brakes, were provided by the Army or Navy and were identified as Government Furnished Equipment, or GFE. The aircraft unit costs presented in this book are mostly those billed by Curtiss to the Navy as listed in Navy contract figures, and do not include GFE. In some cases, especially with company-owned prototypes, the Navy bought the entire aircraft, power plant and all, and also paid the development costs.

Characteristics And Performance

Except where otherwise noted, the figures for Navy Curtiss Hawk characteristics and performance have been taken from official contemporary Navy documents - "Characteristics and Performance- U.S. Navy Aircraft". These figures do not always agree with corresponding figures released by Curtiss, especially in the areas of aircraft weight and performance. In the l920s the Navy noted that the difference between "East Coast" and "West Coast" aviation gasoline had a notable effect on aircraft performance. For comparison between nearly identical U.S. Army and Navy "Hawks", it should be noted that the Army rated the Curtiss D-12C engine at 435 hp at 2,300 rpm while the Navy rated the same engine at 400 hp at 2,200 rpm.

It should also be noted that as aircraft designs advanced, acquiring more weight, power and systems complexity, it took longer to test and approve prototypes. It also took longer to get the inevitable "new airplane bugs" out of production models in service. One, the last of the Navy Curtiss Hawk biplanes, was never successfully debugged and was withdrawn from service within a year because of these problems.

Power Plant Designations

Until the late 1920s, the engines used in American military aircraft were identified by the manufacturer's designations - Curtiss D-12, Pratt & Whitney R-1340, Wright J-5, etc. Progressive variants of these engines were identified by letter - D-12C, R-1340B, etc. On 1 February 1928, in a rare bit of inter-service cooperation, the U.S. Army and Navy agreed to standardize aircraft engine designations.

Engines were then identified as to type by a letter - V for Vee, R for Radial, etc., followed

During 1924, Curtiss redesigned the TS-1 as the F4C-1. The main differences were an all-metal structure and raising the lower wing to the underside of the fuselage. The aircraft retained the 200 hp Lawrance J-1 air-cooled radial engine used on the TS-1. (Curtiss, T-2722)

This was the second of the R2C-1s (BuNo A-6692) Navy racing aircraft. It was fitted with a 507 hp Curtiss D-12A engine and won the Pulitzer Race in 1923. It also set a World's Speed Record of 266.50 mph. The aircraft had shock absorbers built into the wheels of the rigid, wire-braced landing gear. (USN)

by a number giving the displacement to the nearest five cubic inches. The D-12 then became the V-1150 and the J-5 became the R-790. The R-1340 did not change since it already used the system.

After the Navy issued its version of the directive, it promptly revised it to apply to radial engines only. The V-1150 then reverted to its D-12 designation and remained so to the end of its Navy service in Curtiss F6C-3s in l932. By 1933, sequential development of military engines was identified by dash numbers, which were divided between the services. The Army used odd numbers, -l, -3, -5, etc., while the Navy used even dash numbers.

Boeing - Curtiss Competition

Curtiss and Boeing appeared to be neck-and-neck competitors for U.S. Army and Navy fighter business. From 1925 through l933, they supplied almost all of the single-seat fighters to both services.

Actually, the competition was not a true win-or-lose affair. It was the policy of both services to rely on two sources for several types of aircraft, so it was not a case of choosing one design over another. This book will show that when the Navy placed a production order with Curtiss, it also placed another of nearly similar size for a corresponding Boeing model. After the F7C-l Seahawk of l928; however, Curtiss sold no more single-seat fighters to the Navy in squadron strength until 1932. Boeing monopolized the Navy single-seat fighter market with its F4B series until Curtiss re-entered the field with the F11C Goshawk.

The competition was for a very small market by present-day standards. In 1926, the Navy and Marine Corps had only two regular fighter squadrons each. By 1933, these had grown to six for the Navy and three for the Marines. In 1937, the last year of full-squadron use of Navy Hawks, the Navy had five designated fighter squadrons and three single-seat bomber squadrons, two using Boeing F4B-4s and one using Curtiss BFC-2s. The Marines were down to two fighter squadrons.

Reading squadron numbers from aircraft photos gives the impression of more, but such is not the case. Squadron redesignations resulted in new numbers for the same organizations and some Navy fighter squadrons were redesignated as bomber squadrons while still using the same F-designated aircraft as bombers.

Development

F6C-1

F6C-2

F6C-3

F6C-4

F7C-1

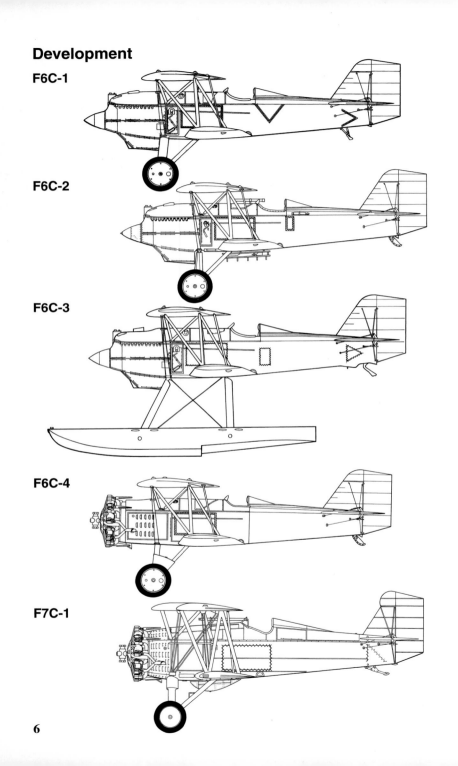

F9C-2

F11C-2

BFC-2

BF2C-1

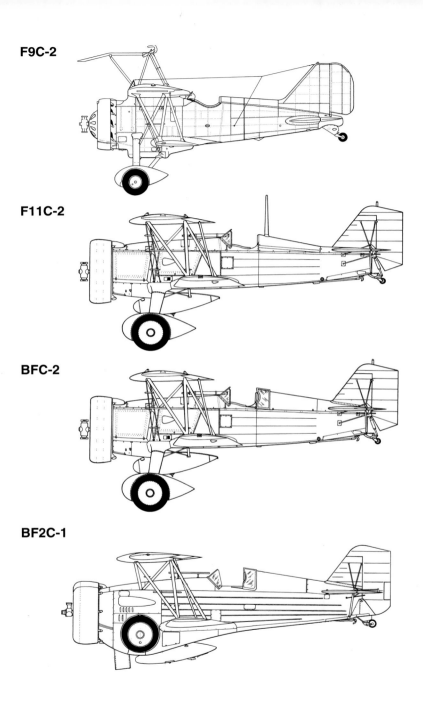

F6C Hawk Series

After the U.S. Army ordered the Curtiss P-l Hawk, powered by the 430 hp Curtiss D-l2 water-cooled engine, the Navy quickly ordered nine near-duplicates as land-based fighters under the designation F6C-1 (Curtiss Model 34C). These aircraft differed from the Army P-1s in minor details of Navy finish requirements and over-all coloring. The F6C-l had a length of 22 feet 9 15/16 inches, a wingspan of 31 feet 6 inches and a height of 8 feet ten inches. The empty weight was 2,059 pounds and loaded weight was 2,802 pounds. It had a top speed at sea level 163.2 mph, a service ceiling of 21,700 feet and a range of 382 miles. Later variants of the F6C were modified to operate from aircraft carriers and others reflected the Navy's changing power plant and deck-landing requirements. Still others were withdrawn from squadron service for test work and for conversion to closed-course pylon racers. As was typical of military aircraft kept in production through several variants, the F6C series gained weight and lost performance as the design progressed.

F6C-1

Only the first five of the nine F6C-1s ordered (BuNos 6969/6972) were delivered as F6C-1s (the last four were modified to F6C-2 standards). Since they were not equipped for carrier operations, three were assigned to Navy Fighter Squadron VF-2 at San Diego, California. Later, two F6C-1s (BuNos A-6970 and A-6972) were upgraded to F6C-3 standards and were redesignated. The first F6C-l became the F6C-4 prototype and later the XF6C-5.

The corresponding Boeing model was the FB-1, with ten being ordered (BuNos A-6884/6893) as navalized versions of the Army PW-9. As land-based fighters, most of the FB-1s went to the U.S. Marines.

The F6C-1 featured a welded steel tube fuselage with tie rod bracing and aluminum-frame ailerons and tail surfaces. The tapered wings (designed at the request of the Army by Curtiss

The Navy ordered nine equivalents of the Army P-1 Hawk under the designation F6C-1. These were intended to be land based fighters for the Marine Corps and were not equipped for carrier operations. This is the first F6C-1 (BuNo A-6968) undergoing testing at Naval Air Station, Anacostia, Virginia. (USN via Kenn C. Rust)

The third F6C-1 (BuNo A-6970) was also tested on twin wooden floats built by Curtiss. The aircraft was equipped with a patented Curtiss-Reid twisted-metal propeller. This float installation was standardized and was similar to those used on subsequent F6C series aircraft. (Curtiss, T-2893)

engineer George Page to replace the straight wings of the PW-8, creating the XPW-8B/P-1, prototype) used two parallel wooden box spars with wood-truss ribs and the new Clark Y airfoil. The normal fuel load was 150 U.S. gallons housed in a single fuselage tank. This could be supplemented by a fifty gallon auxiliary tank with a flat top that attached to the aircraft under the fuselage. The F6C-1 carried the prevailing Navy standard armament of two .30 caliber Browning machine guns under the forward turtledeck firing through the propeller arc. Delivery of F6C-ls to the Navy began in September of 1925.

In 1926, the F6C-1s of VF-2 participated in Navy experiments in dive bombing. A 45-degree dive was initiated at a height of 2,500 feet, with bomb release and pull-up at 400 feet. These experiments proved to be highly successful. Another F6C-1 seaplane (BuNo A-6970) won the 1926 Curtiss Marine Trophy Race on 14 May with a speed of l30.94 mph.

After serving briefly with VF-2, two unconverted F6C-ls were transferred to Marine Fighter Squadron VF-l0M during 1927 to serve as land based fighters. At the time, the squadron was also based at San Diego.

Unit costs for the F6C-ls were not available, but the Navy was paying $10,490 for D-l2 engines at the time the last F6C-1 (BuNo A-6971) was retired in February of 1931, with 500 hours and one minute of flight time. The aircraft had served with Navy squadrons VF-2 and VF-6 and Marine Fighter Squadron VF-9M at Quantico, Virginia. The high-time F6C-l, with 512 hours 25 minutes, was BuNo A-6969 which crashed on 20 July l929.

This was the last F6C-1 in service with VF-2 and carried the unit insignia on the fuselage side forward of the codes. The overall Silver aircraft had a Red tail and Chrome Yellow upper wing. It also lacked the wheel covers normally carried on the F6C-1. (Hasse via SDAM)

F6C-2

At the Navy's request, the last four F6C-ls were modified at the factory to become F6C-2s (BuNos 6973/6976, Curtiss Model 34D). The F6C-2 differed from the F6C-1 in a number of ways. The aircraft were structurally reinforced to withstand hard arrested landings, hook guides were installed between the landing gear struts and an old-fashioned rigid landing gear with a rubber shock cord wound around the axle for shock absorbing was installed. The tail skid was moved to the rear and its shock absorber (rubber cord in tension) was replaced by rubber discs in compression as used on the F6C-1.

The corresponding Boeing model was a pair of FB-2 (BuNos A-6984 and A-6985) which were FB-l airframes modified for shipboard operations.

The weight increases in the F6C series began with the F6C-2. The empty weight increased

This was the second F6C-1 (BuNo 6969) built. The aircraft was assigned to VF-2 based at NAS North Island, San Diego, California. During this time period, the squadron was experimenting with different markings. The wing markings identified the unit (2), type (F - fighter) and aircraft within the unit (1). The Red circle and Red fuselage band identified the aircraft as belonging to a section leader. (Hasse via SDAM)

These three F6C-1s were retained by VF-2 after the other two aircraft were converted to F6C-3 standards. The squadron was unique in that most of its pilots were enlisted men, not officers (officers served as section leaders). Later the unit changed its insignia to that of the rating badge of a Chief Petty Officer and became known as the Flying Chiefs. (Hasse via SDAM)

The F6C-2 was a conversion of the F6C-1 with a new high impact landing gear to allow it to operate from aircraft carriers. The two forward steel-tube landing gear struts were fabric covered and resembled a single strut. During the F6C-2's period of service, the Navy did not carry the national insignia on the underside of the lower wing. (Curtiss T-2988)

Fuselage Development

F6C-1

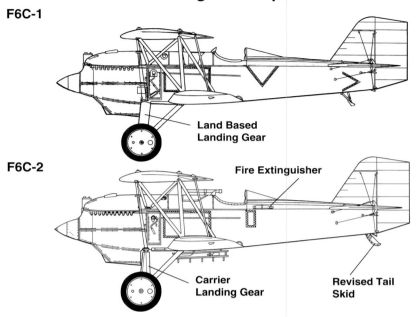

Land Based
Landing Gear

F6C-2

Fire Extinguisher

Carrier
Landing Gear

Revised Tail
Skid

to 2,125 pounds and the gross weight increased to 2,868 pounds. The aircraft's performance suffered accordingly; the top speed dropped to 150 mph but the service ceiling, according to Navy figures, increased to 22,700 feet. Range at cruising speed fell to 362 miles.

Three of the F6C-2s, delivered in November of 1925, were assigned, along with three F6C-

The second F6C-2 (BuNo A-6974) shortly after delivery to VF-2. TH light tone of the Red tail stripe. the dark tone of the Blue stripe and very light tone of the Chrome Yellow upper wing was due to the fact that the film used was Panchromatic with a Yellow filter, a new film type just coming into use. (USN via W. T. Larkins)

The F6C-2 had a redesigned landing gear and revised tail skid. This aircraft is also equipped with a fifty gallon under fuselage fuel tank . The cylinder behind the cockpit is a Pyrene fire extinguisher. The engine starting hand crank was stored in a bracket built into the side of the fuselage just behind the engine. (Curtiss T-2987)

ls and four FB-ls, to VF-2 in San Diego. This squadron was unique in that the majority of its pilots were enlisted men with the rank of Chief Petty Officer. Commissioned officers were the leaders of each three-plane flight section. Late in 1926 the squadron's insignia was changed from a shield over crossed machine guns to a shield containing the rating badge of a

The Red tail on this F6C-2 of VF-2 appears very dark due to the fact that this was shot with Orthochromatic film, the more common type in use at the time. This film made the Chrome Yellow upper wing appear much darker. The aircraft has had the wheel covers removed, (Hasse via SDAM)

9

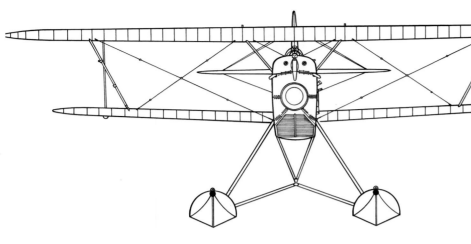

Specification
Curtiss F6C-3 Hawk

Wingspan..31 feet 6 inches (9.6 m**)**
Length...22 feet 9 15/16 inches (6.93 m) - Land
25 feet 5 inches (7.7 m) - Sea
Height...8 feet 10 inches (2.6 m) - Land
10 feet 81/2 inches (3.2 m) - Sea
Empty Weight..2,162 pounds (1,360 kg) - Land
2,514 pounds (1,140 kg) - Sea
Maximum Weight.......................................2,963 pounds (1,344 kg) - Land
3,316 pounds (1,504 kg) - Sea
Powerplant...One 400hp Curtiss D-12 liquid-cooled engine
Armament...Two .30 caliber machine guns or one.30 caliber
and one .50 caliber machine gun.
Speed...153.6 mph (247.1 kph) - Land
155 mph (249,4 kph) - Sea
Service Ceiling...20,300 feet (6,187 m) - Land
19,100 feet (5,821 m) - Sea
Range...341 miles (548 km) - Land
331 miles (532.6 km) - Sea
Crew..One

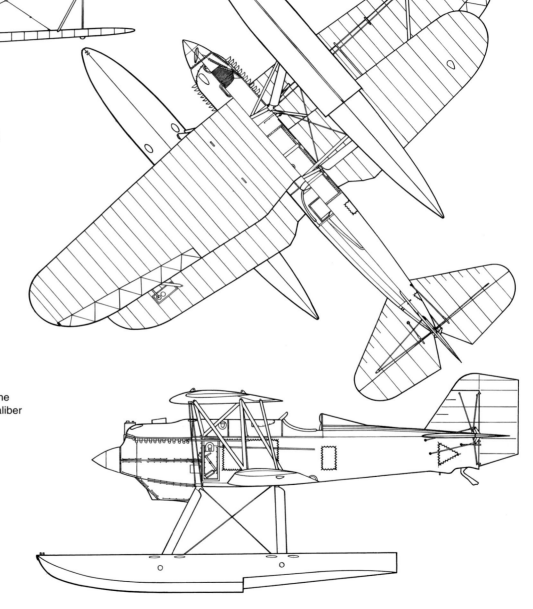

The second F6C-2 (BuNo A-6974) displays the original VF-2 squadron insignia and is equipped with a bomb rack under the fuselage. During this period of Navy unit markings, the fuselage band, identifying section leaders, was not centered on the central letter of the unit code marking. VF-2 later became VF-6B during 1927. (USN)

Chief Petty Officer.

One F6C-2 (BuNo A-6973) was assigned to the USS LANGLEY (CV-1), the Navy's first aircraft carrier . This assignment was to the ship itself, not to a squadron aboard the ship. As such, it carried the lettering USS LANGLEY - 6 on the fuselage sides. Following service with VF-2 well into l928, the shore-based F6C-2s were transferred to the Marines.

The high-time F6C-2 (BuNo A-6974) was retired in June of 1930 with 359 hours 3l minutes of flying time. The last F6C-2 (BuNo A-6973) retired in July of 1931, after logging 345 hours 15 minutes.

The first F6C-2 (BuNo A-6973) was assigned to the aircraft carrier USS LANGLEY(CV-1), not to a squadron aboard the ship, and carried the Red-White-Blue diagonal band that identified LANGLEY's aircraft. The hooks on the cross-axle engaged the longitudinal deck wires. (USN via Ken C. Rust)

F6C-3

Experience gained with the two upgraded F6C-2s resulted in an order for thirty-five carrier-based F6C-3s (BuNos A-7128/7162, Curtiss Model 34E), which were generally the equivalent of the Army P-lA Hawk (Model 34G). This time the Army Hawk followed the Navy's lead. Navy-initiated refinements to the F6C-3 were incorporated into the P-lA, which had a fuselage three inches longer than previous Hawks and used the improved D-12C engine. Again, weight increased and performance suffered.

The F6C-3 reflected the Navy's concern for heavier armament for its fighters. Like earlier Army Hawks, F6C-3s were given the provision for replacing the starboard .30 caliber machine gun with a Browning .50 caliber gun as an alternate installation. This optional armament installation was to remain standard to the end of Navy biplane fighter production. The F6C-3 could also carry bombs on a rack installed on the underfuselage fuel tank fittings.

The F6C-3s used as shipboard fighters were initially fitted with F6C-2 landing gear and tail skids, but these were replaced in service by a later type used on the production F6C-4. F6C-3s assigned to land-based Marine Corps squadrons were fitted with F6C-l style landing gear. During their service careers, F6C-3s underwent a number of tail skid changes and provision was made for the installation of twin floats in place of the wheel landing gear. This configuration was flight tested on F6C-1s and F6C-2s, and one Navy squadron, VB-1B (formerly VF-5) operated briefly on floats during 1928.

Equivalent Boeing models were twenty-seven FB-5s (BuNos A-7101/7127) that were major

Fuselage Development

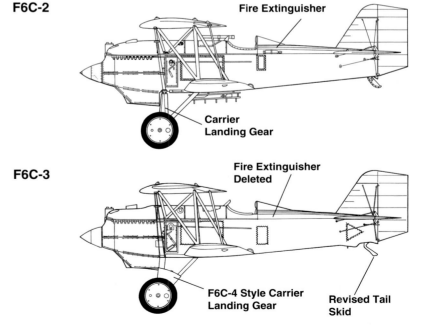

F6C-2

Fire Extinguisher

Carrier Landing Gear

F6C-3

Fire Extinguisher Deleted

F6C-4 Style Carrier Landing Gear

Revised Tail Skid

The equivalent Boeing model to the F6C-3 was the FB-5 with a 520 hp Packard 2A-1500 engine. These FB-5s, of VF-I and VF-6, were Navy entries in the 1927 National Air Races at Spokane, Washington. (Author's Collection)

Landing Gear Development

This was the first production F6C-3 (BuNo A-7I28). The F6C-3s were delivered with F6C-2 main landing gear and tail skids. Later, these were replaced by F6C-4 type landing gear for carrier-based aircraft and with F6C-1 type landing gear for land-based U.S. Marine Corps aircraft. (Curtiss 3147-8)

A Marine Corps F6C-3 (BuNo A-7I46) on the grass at Marine Corps Air Station Quantico, Virginia during March of I929. Markings are Marine Corps standard for the time, with F-for-fighter in a small circle within the unit designator. The aircraft had F6C-1 style landing gear and a Red spinner, headrest and wheel covers. (USMC via W. F. Gemeinhardt)

F6C-1

Tripod Type Land Based Landing Gear Used On F6C-1 And USMC F6C-3/4s

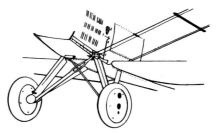

F6C-2

Initial Carrier Landing Gear Used on F6C-2/3

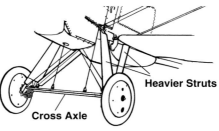

Heavier Struts

Cross Axle

F6C-4/3

Late Carrier Landing Gear Used On F6C-4s And Retrofitted To F6C-3s

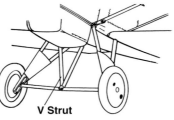

V Strut

A F6C-3 (BuNo A-7137) of VF-5 Red Rippers on the flight deck of USS LEXINGTON (CV-2). During early 1928, the aircraft model designation of Navy aircraft was added to the upper portion of the rudder with the name of the manufacturer below it. The letters were White against Red and blue and Black against White. (USN)

revisions of the basic PW-9/FB design, using the new 525 hp Packard 1A-1500 water-cooled engine. All were carrier-based.

Delivery of F6C-3s began in October of 1926, with unit costs of $12,938. By this time the Navy was paying $9,500 for Curtiss D-12 engines. Eighteen F6C-3s were delivered to

In July of 1928, VF-5 was redesignated as a bomber squadron, VB-1B and attached to the Battle Force. The squadron remained home based on the LEXINGTON, but operated for a brief period on floats. The E for Excellence marking on the nose was for bombing. Even though it was on floats, BuNo A-7144 retained its tail skid. The tail color was Yellow. The aircraft carried no Black leader stripe, even though aircraft 10 was the leader of the fourth section. (USN)

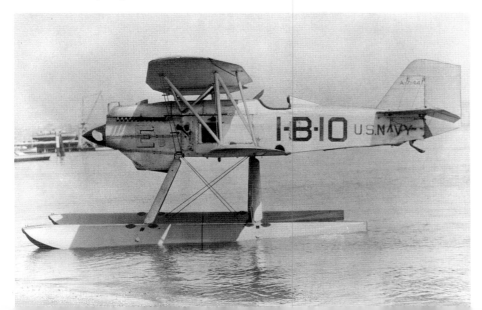

A Yellow-tailed F6C-3 (BuNo A-7140) of VB-1B aboard USS LEXINGTON carries an over-size, and faded, unit designator on top of the wing facing in the proper direction. The two openings on the upper portion of the nose are the gun ports for the two machine guns. The F6C-3 could carry either two .30 caliber guns or one .30 and one .50 caliber gun. (Hasse via SDAM)

Fighter Squadron Five (VF-5) at Norfolk, Virginia. This squadron was soon to become famous as The Red Rippers. They went aboard the newly commissioned USS LEXINGTON (CV-2), the Navy's second aircraft carrier, and accompanied the ship when it transferred to the West Coast.

In July of 1928, VF-5 was redesignated as a bombing squadron, VB-1B, although it retained its F6C-3s. The suffix letter B added to a squadron designation (beginning in July of 1928), did not indicate the use of fighter aircraft as bombers, but rather that the squadron was assigned to the Fleet Battle Force. Squadrons with S-suffixes were assigned to the Scouting Force. VB-1B reverted to VF-5B in 1930, but by then they were not flying Hawks.

In 1927, other F6C-3s were delivered to land-based Marine fighter squadrons. Both VF-8M (formerly VF-1M) and VF-9M, based at Marine Corps Air Station Quantico, Virginia received F6C-3s. In keeping with the Navy's new policy of using only air-cooled engines in its fleet-based aircraft, the F6C-3s, along with the FB-5s were withdrawn from fleet service and passed to shore commands, such as the Marines.

The last F6C-3 (BuNo A-7146) was grounded in July of 1932. It was also the high-time F6C-3, with a total of 1037 hours 9 minutes of flying time.

This was the cockpit of a F6C-3. The two guns are both .30 caliber Browning air cooled machine guns. The flight and engine instruments were distributed over three separate panels. The lower center panel had the airspeed (center), altimeter (right) and an tachometer (left). (Curtiss 3157-8)

The first F6C-3 used for racing was the first F6C-3 built (BuNo A-7128). While under test at Naval Air Station Anacostia, Virginia, it became a reserve aircraft for the Navy 1926 Schneider Cup racing team. Pressed into service, it placed fourth at 136.95 mph. (National Archives)

F6C-3 Racers

Both land and seaplane variants of the F6C-3 were used by the Navy and Marines for closed-course racing from 1926 to 1930. Some were stock aircraft, while others were extensively modified.

The first F6C-3 racer (BuNo A-7128) was used as a reserve aircraft for the Navy's 1926 Schneider Cup Trophy Racing team. Since the United States had won the 1925 event, the 1926 race was held in the United States at Norfolk, Virginia, on 13 November. The F6C-3 flew because the Navy's other pure racing aircraft had been eliminated.

The D-12A engine was modified to produce up to 507 hp and the under fuselage fuel tank was enlarged to allow the aircraft to carry enough fuel to cover the 213 mile closed course at full throttle. The F6C-3 placed fourth to higher powered pure racing designs at a speed 136.95 mph.

Curtiss Marine Trophy

The Curtiss Marine Trophy Race was established in 1913 by Glenn Curtiss as an annual closed-course race for U.S. Navy seaplanes. Since this was usually run as a single isolated event unconnected to the other major race meets, it received little attention from the public and is virtually unknown, even to present-day air race historians.

F6C-3s participated from 1926 through the final running in 1930. They won in 1928 and 1930, with speeds of 157.6 and 164.08 mph, respectively. It is a sad commentary that in spite of all the great advances in aircraft design during the late 1920s, the fastest seaplane in the Navy, in 1930, was the 1926 production model of a 1924 design.

A F6C-3 (BuNo A-7144) was withdrawn from service and sent to the Naval Aircraft Factory for extensive modification as a racer. Major changes include a low-drag straight-axle landing gear, installation of the radiator inside the fuselage and a rounding of the rear fuselage contours. (Author's Collection)

F6C-6

During the 1920s, both the Army and the Navy participated in closed-course pylon races at such major racing events as the National Air Races. Until 1929, these were strictly all-military races, since there were no civil aircraft capable of competing. Prior to the 1929 National Air Race the Navy sent a F6C-3 (BuNo A-7144) to the Naval Aircraft Factory for an extensive cleanup which was intended to reduce drag and increase its speed.

It is interesting to note, from a political point of view, that the aircraft's technical records make no mention of its racing career. The purpose of the modification was to "evaluate Prestone cooling for normally water-cooled engines," a year after liquid-cooled aircraft had been withdrawn from the fleet.

The conspicuous chin radiator was removed and two smaller core radiators were installed inside the fuselage behind the firewall. Large airscoops, which ran the full height of the fuse-

In its final form BuNo A-7144 was redesignated as the F6C-6 and was fitted with wheel pants for the 1929 National Air Races. In spite of the extensive cleanup and a publicized speed of over 200 mph, its performance was disappointing. The aircraft placed fourth at 153.38 mph. (William F. Yeager)

A Marine Corps F6C-3 (BuNo A-7147) was modified for the 1930 Curtiss Marine Trophy Race, which it won at 164.08 mph. The aircraft had all the cowling fasteners taped over, the fuel tank cap covered by a fairing and the rear fuselage was faired into the belly tank. (USN via San Diego Aerospace Museum)

lage, directed airflow into the cores, and the heated air exhausted through louvers in aluminum side panels at the rear of the cores. The fuselage was rounded out to the rear of the cockpit by adding formers and stringers to the basic structure. The final item was to replace the F6C-l landing gear with a cleaner rigid cross-axle type, fitted with streamlined wheel "pants." This new streamlining feature had first been used on commercial Lockheed designs late in 1928. When first tested in its new form, the Hawk still carried its F6C-3 designation, but this was changed to F6C-6 by the time of the race.

The free-for-all event, in which civil aircraft competed against the military for the first time, was a humiliating defeat for both services. The new Travel Air Model R monoplane, dubbed "The Mystery Ship," won the five-lap fifty mile closed course race at 194.90 mph. The Model R was powered by a Wright J-6-9 (R-975) Whirlwind engine which had a normal rating of 300 hp, but was boosted to 400 hp for the race. Second place, at 186.84 mph, went to the Army's second XP-3A Hawk (serial 28-189) which had a 450 hp R-1340 engine and had been used by the National Advisory Committee for Aeronautics (NACA) for streamlining research. Third place went to a Lockheed Vega cabin monoplane with a 420 hp Wasp engine at 163.44 mph. All three winners featured the new NACA cowling around their radial engines.

The F6C-6, in spite of its extensive cleanup and boosted engine, placed fourth at a disappointing 153.38 mph. The F6C-3 seaplane that had won the 1928 Curtiss Trophy was faster. After the race, the F6C-6 was reconverted to F6C-3 standards, to the extent practicable, and was redesignated as a F6C-3. Its rounded out rear fuselage was retained, however, making it distinctive among surviving F6C-3s.

XF6C-6

For the 1930 race, the Navy made an all-out effort to win the free-for-all unlimited event, now called the Thompson Trophy Race, which was to be held on 1 September. The second Naval Hawk to race against civilians, and the last pylon racer of either service, was a Marine Corps F6C-3 (BuNo A-7147) that had just won the 1930 Curtiss Trophy race. It was sent back to Curtiss in June of 1930 for one of the most extensive modifications ever made to a standard military aircraft and became the XF6C-6. It quickly won the popular name of "Page Navy Racer," because it was to be flown by Marine Captain Arthur Page, winner of the 1930 Curtiss Trophy.

The biplane was converted to a parasol monoplane configuration. The upper wing was retained, but was extensively rebuilt to accommodate wing-surface radiators of the type used on the early 1920s Curtiss racers and the Army PW-8s. To maintain longitudinal balance, the wing was moved far enough aft to keep the new center of lift in line with the center of gravity.

Fuselage modifications were extensive. The cockpit opening was greatly reduced and the sides and underfuselage were rounded out to fair into the new smooth nose cowling that covered a special Curtiss V-1570 Conqueror engine that had been boosted to 770 hp from its normal 600 hp. The final touch was a new single-leg landing gear to replace the original tripod design.

No full Performance tests were made of the racer, which now carried Navy markings and a special Navy Blue and Chrome Yellow color scheme, but its calculated top speed was 250 mph. It was well on its way to proving this when Page was overcome by carbon monoxide fumes and crashed while leading the field on the 17th lap of the 20 lap race. His best lap time was 219.6 mph. This tragedy ended Navy participation in closed-course racing. The Army had abandoned the practice after the 1929 races.

Curtiss Hawk technology benefited from the XF6C-6 modifications; however, since the single leg landing gear was to become a standard feature of the Army P-6E (Model 35B), the export "Hawk II" (Model 47) and the Navy F11C-2/BFC-2 (Model 64A).

The Navy's final effort at air racing was this F6C-3 (BuNo A-7147) which was extensively rebuilt for the 1930 Thompson Trophy Race. It was converted to a monoplane and powered by a 770 hp Curtiss V-1570 engine. The radiators were wing surface types as used on earlier Curtiss racers. The three-piece cockpit coaming was used to reduce the size and drag of the cockpit opening. Marine Captain Page was leading the field (219.6 mph) when he was overcome by carbon monoxide fumes and crashed. (Curtiss T-5987)

F6C-4

When the Navy began to favor new 400 hp and higher air-cooled radial engines for its fleet-based aircraft, it sent the first F6C-1 (BuNo A-6968) back to Curtiss for installation of a Navy-sponsored Pratt & Whitney R-1340 Wasp engine, an air-cooled, nine-cylinder radial that delivered 420 hp at 1,900 rpm at sea level. The aircraft was then redesignated as the F6C-4. Flight tests were begun in August of 1926, and with their satisfactory conclusion, an order was placed for thirty-one production F6C-4s (BuNos A-7393/7423, Curtiss Model 34H). The first production aircraft, fitted with a new high-impact landing gear (initially tested on a F6C-3 during October of 1926), was delivered in March of 1927, and served as a pilot model. As such it was later designated the XF6C-4. Deliveries of the remaining production F6C-4s, which did not have the large propeller spinner of the prototype and pilot models, did not begin until August of 1927.

The air-cooled engine reduced the empty weight of the F6C-4 to 1,980 pounds and the gross weight to 2,785 pounds. The service ceiling rose to 22,900 feet and the sea level top speed was 155 mph. The unit cost of a F6C-4 was $11,808 and the Wasp engine cost the Navy $7,730.

While the F6C-4 was simply an established model with a new engine, the matching Boeing was a new model, the F2B-1. This was a major redesign of the FB series specifically to use the Wasp engine. After testing the XF2B-1 prototype (BuNo A-7385), which first flew in November of 1926, the Navy ordered thirty-two production F2B-1s (BuNos A-7424/7455). As with the F6C-4 prototype, the XF2B-1 featured a large propeller spinner, which was not used on the production models. Although ordered after the F6C-4s, the Boeings were delivered earlier.

The F6C-4s went primarily to the U.S. Marines, and were distributed among VF-1M, VF-9M and VF-10M. VF-2B also operated eight F6C-4s and eight F2B-1s aboard USS LANGLEY into 1930, and even had some F6C-4 mounted on floats for a brief period. In 1930, VF-2B's F6C-4s were transferred to VF-10M based in San Diego, California where they continued to

The first F6C-1 (BuNo A-6968) was returned to Curtiss and fitted at the Navy's request with the new 420 hp Pratt & Whitney R-1340 Wasp air-cooled radial engine under the designation F6C-4. The aircraft was equipped with long bayonet exhaust stacks on each of the nine cylinders. (Arthur Price)

Fuselage Development

F6C-3

D-12 Liquid Cooled Engine

F6C-4

420 hp R-1340 Air-cooled Radial Engine

Revised Tail Skid

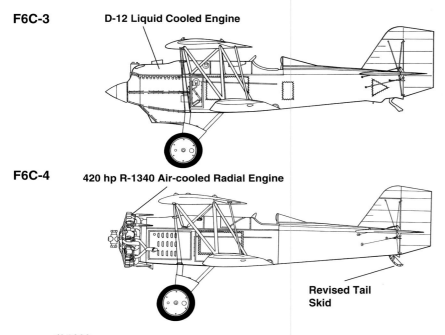

serve until 1932.

In 1930, some Marine F6C-4s were fitted with Townend anti-drag rings around their Pratt & Whitney Wasp engines. These were relatively cheap and light adaptations of the full NACA cowling made famous by the 1929 races and added a few mph to the aircraft's speed without

The first F6C-4 of the production order (BuNo A-7393) was delivered in March of 1927, with a new style of carrier landing gear. Used for test work, BuNo A-7393 was later redesignated as the XF6C-4 and served briefly with Marine Fighter Squadron VF-4M. (Curtiss)

While at Anacostia, this F6C-4 (BuNo A-7403) had its landing gear replaced by floats and was tested as a seaplane. It flew in the 1929 Curtiss Marine Trophy Race. These floats lack water rudders, which had been introduced on the civil market by Edo in 1926. (USN)

the installation and baffling problems of the NACA cowling. The principal drawback of the Townend ring was its interference with the pilot's forward vision.

The last F6C-4 (BuNo A-7398) was classified as worn out and grounded during April of

BuNo A-7403 was reconfigured back to a landplane at Anacostia during 1930 with high-impact carrier landing gear but no arrester hook. Production F6C-4s had the late F6C-3 tail skid, not the F6C-1 type used on the pilot model (BuNo A-7393). This aircraft had non-standard fuselage access panels. (USN)

This land-based F6C-4 (BuNo A-7395) of Marine Fighter Squadron VF-1M, was fitted with F6C-1 landing gear. The F in the unit marking is the same size as the numbers and that the circle, denoting a Marine Corps aircraft, was larger than standard (compair with 10-F-5 below). (USMC via Kenn C. Rust)

This F6C-4 (BuNo A-7404) was a former Navy aircraft turned over to the Marines and fitted with a Townend ring around the engine. The aircraft has a non-regulation star insignia under upper wing, which was exclusive to this squadron. The aircraft carried the squadron insignia on the fin. The manufacturer's name was no longer carried on the rudder. (USN)

This F6C-4 BuNo 7398 (use of the A-prefix had been discontinued by this time) on the ramp at Anacostia on 11 May 1931 was being used as a test bed for the Hamilton-Standard controllable-pitch propeller. The national insignia was carried on the underside of the lower wing by this time. (USN via Joe Christy)

1933, with a total of 855 hours 50 minutes flight time. The high-time F6C-4 (BuNo A-7417) had 1,148 hours 50 minutes of logged flight time.

F6C-4 Variants

The prototype and several production F6C-4s were used as testbeds for a number of power plant experiments, some of which resulted in changes in the aircraft's designation.

F6C-5

After the first F6C-1 (BuNo A-6968) became the prototype F6C-4 powered by a R-1340 Wasp engine, it was later used as a test bed for another Pratt & Whitney radial engine, the slightly larger 525 hp R-1690 Hornet. With this power plant, the aircraftwas redesignated as the F6C-5 (later XF6C-5 after the Navy adopted the X-for-Experimental prefix in 1927). No production order was forthcoming and no F6C Hawk, nor any other Army or Navy fighter ever used the "Hornet" engine.

F6C-4 (Wright-Powered)

One Production F6C-4 (BuNo A-7403) was loaned to the Wright Aeronautical Corporation in 1929 for use as a test bed for the new 300 hp Wright R-975 (J-6-9) Whirlwind engine. In spite of the engine change, the aircraft's designation was not changed, even though this was standard practice. The purpose of the program was to test the new engine in a suitable airframe, not to upgrade the now obsolescent Hawk.

The first F6C-1 (BuNo A-6968) in its final form as the F6C-5 with a Pratt & Whitney R-1690 Hornet radial engine and production F6C-4 landing gear. The letterboard in the foregound was used to identify test aircraft photographed at Naval Air Station (NAS) Anacostia, Virginia. (USN)

The former-Wright powreed XF6C-4 (BuNo A-7403) in the Naval Aircraft Factory where it served as the test-bed for the XF6C-7, which used the experimental inverted Ranger V-770 engine. (NACA)

In using the R-975, this F6C-4 matched the two U.S. Army XP-2l Hawks that had been redesignated from the two XP-3As (serials 25-300 and 28-189) to test the very similar 300 hp Pratt & Whitney R-985 Twin Wasp Jr. engine. This F6C-4 (BuNo A-7403) later became the XF6C-7 prototype.

XF6C-7

Another experimental engine installationwas made to a F6C-4 (BuNo A-7403) resulting in it being redesignated as the XF6C-7. The engine was the new 350 hp inverted Ranger SGV-770, an air-cooled V-l2. The letters S and G in the engine designation stood for supercharged and geared. Ranger hoped to get high power from a relatively small displacement by running the engine at a higher speed than contemporary engines; i.e., 2,400 rpm compared to 2,000 rpm for the 300 hp P&W R-985 Wasp Jr. Since such a speed was impractical for the propeller, the engine was geared down at a ratio of 1.32:l. Because of the spur gear, which had been added to an engine that had been originally been designed for direct drive, the propeller turned left-hand which was opposite of standard American practice.

The engine changes were made at the Naval Aircraft Factory in l932. Since the aircraft was to serve only as a test bed for the engine, no performance figures were recorded and the original F6C-4 designation, painted on the aircraft's rudder, were not even changed. With the V-770 installed, the XF6C-7s resembled the U.S Army XP-l7 (the first P-l Hawk [serial 25-410]) which was modified to test the larger but otherwise very similar 480 hp Wright V-l460 engine. The XF6C-7 was reconverted to F6C-4 standards after finishing the test program and returned to normal operations.

The V-770 was not a satisfactory engine at the time, and in fact, it was never truly successful. Improvements by Ranger encouraged the Navy to order it for the prototype Curtiss S03C-l Seagull in May of l938. By that time the engine was delivering 450 hp at 3,000 rpm (520 for takeoff at 3,150 rpm). The Navy ordered large numbers of Seagulls, but a combination of aircraft and power plant problems led to their being withdrawn from fleet service after a short period.

This F6C-4 (BuNo A-7403) was loaned to the Wright Aeronautical Corporation as a test bed for the new Wright R-975 Whirlwind radial engine. It was fitted with a longer nose section, needed to balance the lighter engine. The new nose was faired in with sheet metal that covered the lower ends of the center section struts. (F.H. Dean)

F7C Seahawk

In December of 1927 the Navy initiated a fly-off design competition for new Pratt & Whitney Wasp powered float fighter. Both the F6C-l and F6C-2 had been tested as seaplanes and had proven that the Hawk could operate on floats. While the F6C-3 was yet to operate as a float fighter in squadron strength, it too would find operational use as a float fighter. The new design was to be capable of operations both as land based and as single-float seaplanes. It was intended that it would replace the Vought FU-l seaplane catapult fighters that were stationed aboard battleships. Three manufacturers, Boeing, Curtiss and Eberhard, responded and entered company owned prototypes.

XF7C-1

The new Curtiss (Model 43) prototype had nothing in common with the F6C series except the required Pratt & Whitney Wasp air-cooled radial engine as used in the F6C-4. The fuselage used riveted steel and aluminum tubing, similar to the contemporary Curtiss Falcon two-seater instead of welded steel, and the upper wing was swept back outboard of a straight center section, also similar to the Falcon. The chord was constant over the full span and the airfoil section was the Curtiss C-72. A commonly held belief, thanks to a widely-distributed early Curtiss publicity photo that showed the upper wing leading edge-on, was that the upper wing was originally straight, not swept. This is not so, the outboard wing panels were swept

The prototype Seahawk, known as the "Curtiss Navy Fighter," on the ramp at the Curtiss factory on 28 February 1927. The aircraft had shock absorbers built into the wheels of the rigid-truss landing gear. (Curtiss T-3230)

The prototype Seahawk was tested on a single float landing gear during the three-way design competition held in April of 1927. The large propeller spinner was used only briefly and only on the prototype. (USN)

The Eberhard XF2G-1 lost out in the competition to the Boeing and Curtiss prototypes. An odd feature of the XF2G-1 was that the upper wing was swept back while the lower wing was swept forward. (USN)

20

The prototype Seahawk was modified to production standard and was redesignated the XF7C-1. The aircraft had long ailerons on the upper wing extending inboard to the center section, the aileron actuator strut was located at mid-span, and the spreader bar/cross axle on the landing gear had holes in it for carrier deck alignment hooks. (Curtiss)

from the start.

An unusual feature of the new prototype was the landing gear. Instead of rubber discs in compression as on the F6Cs and Army Hawks, the shock absorbers used on the prototype were spring units built into each wheel, similar to the type used on some of the early 1920s

The XF7C-1 on the grass at the NACA facility for engine cowling tests. The fuselage ahead of the cockpit has been rounded out so that the engine cowling extends to the rear of the forward landing gear strut and covers a portion of it. (NACA)

The XF7C-1 was assigned to Experimental Squadron VX-1 at NAS Hampton Roads, Virginia during March of 1932. The aircraft has had an arrester hook installed and the BuNo has had the A prefix deleted and the X-prefix was also deleted from the model designation. (USN)

Curtiss racers. The landing gear struts formed a rigid divided-axle welded steel tube truss. This landing gear was used on the prototype only, and it had provision for a crossbar that supported the alignment hooks that were used to engage the longitudinal guide wires then in use on Navy carriers.

Curtiss named the new fighter the Seahawk. Although the prototype was company-owned, it was known that it would be officially designated F7C-l if purchased by the Navy, so that designation was painted on the rudder, along with other unofficial lettering that read, "Curtiss (in trademark script) Navy Fighter." The first flight of the Seahawk was on 28 February 1927.

The Eberhard was eliminated from the competition and both the Boeing and Curtiss entries were sent back to their factories for improvements that included new wings of increased span and wing area. The Boeing prototype originally had tapered wings like the FB series, but ended up with constant-chord wings, having the upper wing swept back similar to the Seahawk wing.

The revised Curtiss, now officially designated XF7C-1, won a production order for seventeen aircraft. When that contract was awarded, on 28 August 1927, the prototype was accepted as the first article on the contract and was assigned BuNo A-7653. As a single prototype, the cost was high - $82,450 complete.

The XF7C-l was used mainly for experimental work, and late in its career was fitted with an arrester hook for tests on the simulated carrier deck at Naval Air Station (NAS) Hampton Roads, Virginia. It was also loaned to the NACA for tests of the new NACA cowling. Mounted on floats, it won the l929 Curtiss Marine Trophy with a speed of 162.52 mph. It also served briefly with Marine Fighter Squadrons VF-5M and VF-9M during two separate assignments at Marine Corps Air Station (MCAS) Quantico, Virginia. It was damaged beyond repair at Quantico on 15 May l932, and was stricken from the inventory with a total Navy flight time of 527 hours 6 minutes.

F7C-1

By the time the seventeen production F7C-1s (BuNos A-7654/7670, Curtiss Model 43A) were ordered, the concept of flying seaplane fighters from battleships had been abandoned, so the F7C-1s were delivered as landplanes, but were not equipped for carrier operations.

Deliveries began during November of 1928, with eleven going directly to Marine Fighter Squadron VF-5M (later VF-9M) at MCAS Quantico, Virginia. The remaining six joined them after brief Navy non-squadron use. One (BuNo A-7655) was held at the factory for experimental work and was not delivered until 24 June 1929.

The production F7C-1 differed from the prototype mainly in the entirely new landing gear. This landing gear had oleo-shook absorbers in the front struts and was of the divided-axle type landing gear configuration. In September of 1929, the longitudinal deck wires of aircraft carriers were eliminated. With their elimination, carrier-based aircraft were fitted with wheel brakes and small hard-rubber tail wheels. Although not used on carriers, the production F7C-1s were fitted with brakes, but never did acquire tail wheels. Quantity production brought the unit price, apart from GFE, down to $17,111.

The matching Boeing design was the F3B-l, which started a five-year ascendancy of Boeing over Curtiss for single-seat Navy fighter contracts. There were seventy-three F3B-1s (A-7675/7691/7708/7763), again with the modified prototype becoming the first article of the production contract with BuNo A-7674. These were all carrier-based landplanes and served Navy squadrons VB-1B and VF-3B on USS LEXINGTON and with VF-28 on the new USS SARATOGA (CV-3).

The last F7C-l remaining on active duty (BuNo A-7661) was grounded in August of 1933. This was also the high-time Seahawk, with 934 hours 04 minutes flight time in her log book.

The second production F7C-l (BuNo A-7655) on the grass at the Curtiss factory on 28 November 1928. The production F7C-1 differed from the prototype in having revised landing gear and a belly fuel tank. The dark area above the lower wing root is the canvas container for the emergency flotation bags, one on each side of the fuselage. (Curtiss T-4024)

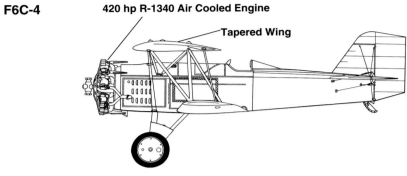

F6C-4

420 hp R-1340 Air Cooled Engine

Tapered Wing

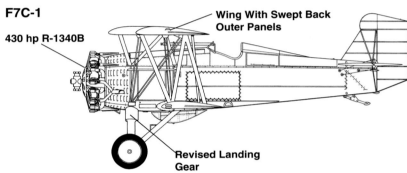

F7C-1

Wing With Swept Back Outer Panels

430 hp R-1340B

Revised Landing Gear

The second production F7C-1 was used to test an experimental tandem-blade propeller during December of 1928. The aircraft had no service designation, U.S. Navy or U.S. Marines, painted on fuselage, as was normal practice. (Curtiss T-4141)

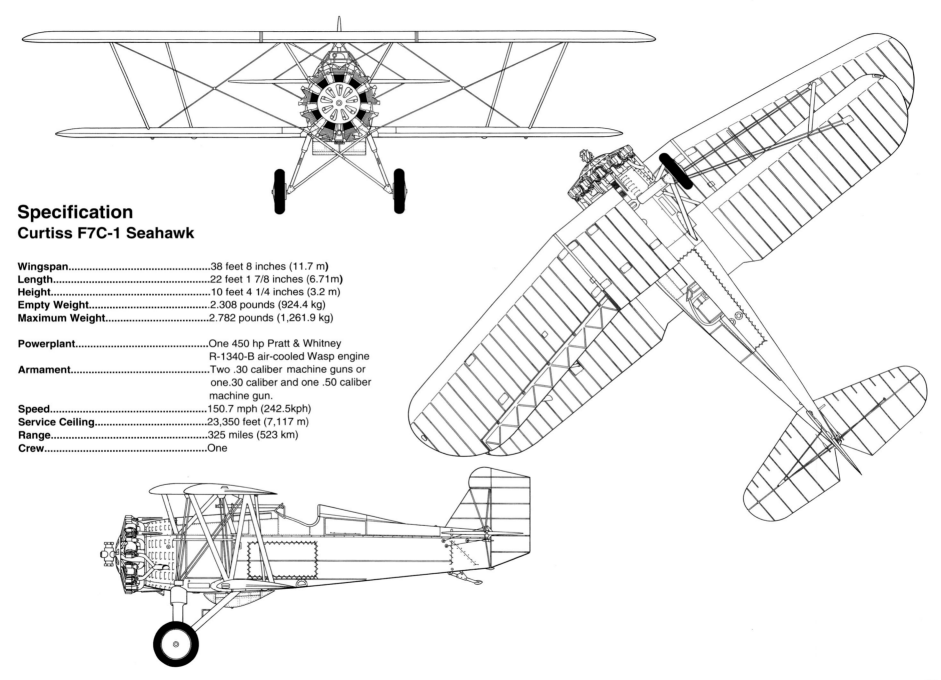

Specification
Curtiss F7C-1 Seahawk

Wingspan	38 feet 8 inches (11.7 m)
Length	22 feet 1 7/8 inches (6.71m)
Height	10 feet 4 1/4 inches (3.2 m)
Empty Weight	2.308 pounds (924.4 kg)
Maximum Weight	2.782 pounds (1,261.9 kg)
Powerplant	One 450 hp Pratt & Whitney R-1340-B air-cooled Wasp engine
Armament	Two .30 caliber machine guns or one.30 caliber and one .50 caliber machine gun.
Speed	150.7 mph (242.5kph)
Service Ceiling	23,350 feet (7,117 m)
Range	325 miles (523 km)
Crew	One

This F7C-1 (BuNo 7661) was one of several fitted with Townend anti-drag rings around their engines late in their USMC service. This was the last Seahawk in service and was also the high-time F7C-1. (Author)

(Top/Bottom) This standard production F7C-1 (BuNo A-7656) was modified with a set of experimental leading edge slats installed on the outer panels of the upper wing during February of 1929. It was the first aircraft to be fitted with automatic leading edge slots, which were intended to give the aircraft a slower landing speed, making it safer to land on carrier decks. (Curtiss T-4219)

A F7C-1 (BuNo 7670) of VF-9M during 1931. The unit markings on the fuselage are non-standard, a practice common to several USMC squadrons in the early 1930s. The A-prefix of the BuNo was deleted late in 1930, but the name CURTISS on rudder was not eliminated until late 1931 or early 1932. (Fred Bamberger Collection)

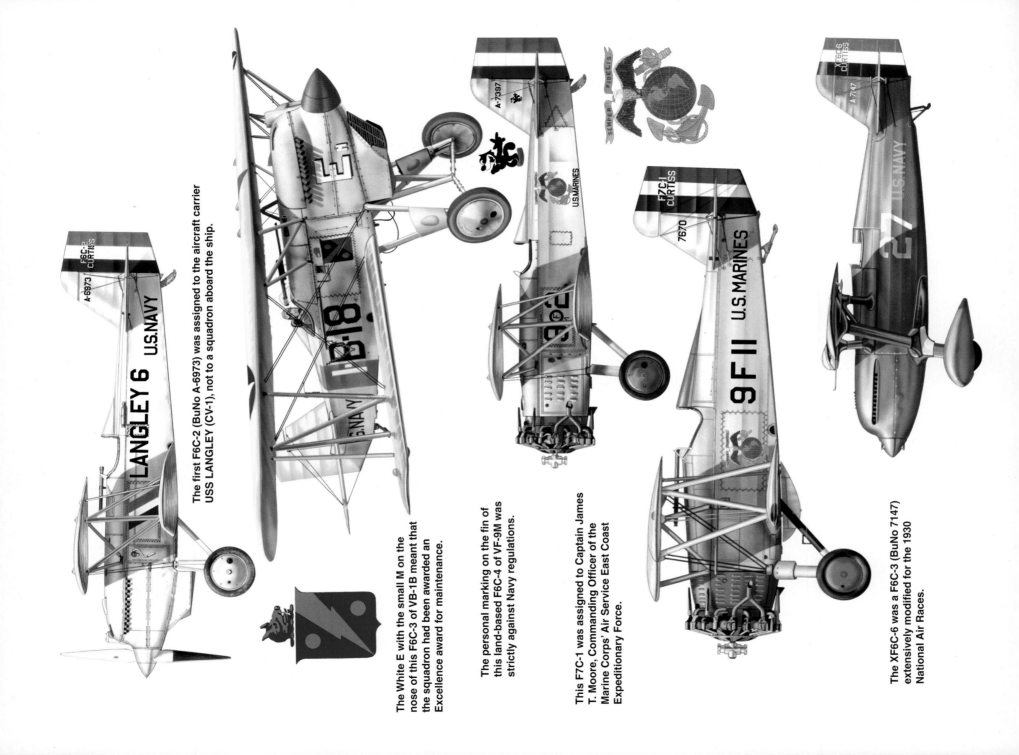

LANGLEY 6 U.S.NAVY

The first F6C-2 (BuNo A-6973) was assigned to the aircraft carrier USS LANGLEY (CV-1), not to a squadron aboard the ship.

The White E with the small M on the nose of this F6C-3 of VB-1B meant that the squadron had been awarded an Excellence award for maintenance.

The personal marking on the fin of this land-based F6C-4 of VF-9M was strictly against Navy regulations.

This F7C-1 was assigned to Captain James T. Moore, Commanding Officer of the Marine Corps' Air Service East Coast Expeditionary Force.

The XF6C-6 was a F6C-3 (BuNo 7147) extensively modified for the 1930 National Air Races.

SEMPER FIDELIS

9 F II U.S. MARINES

U.S. NAVY

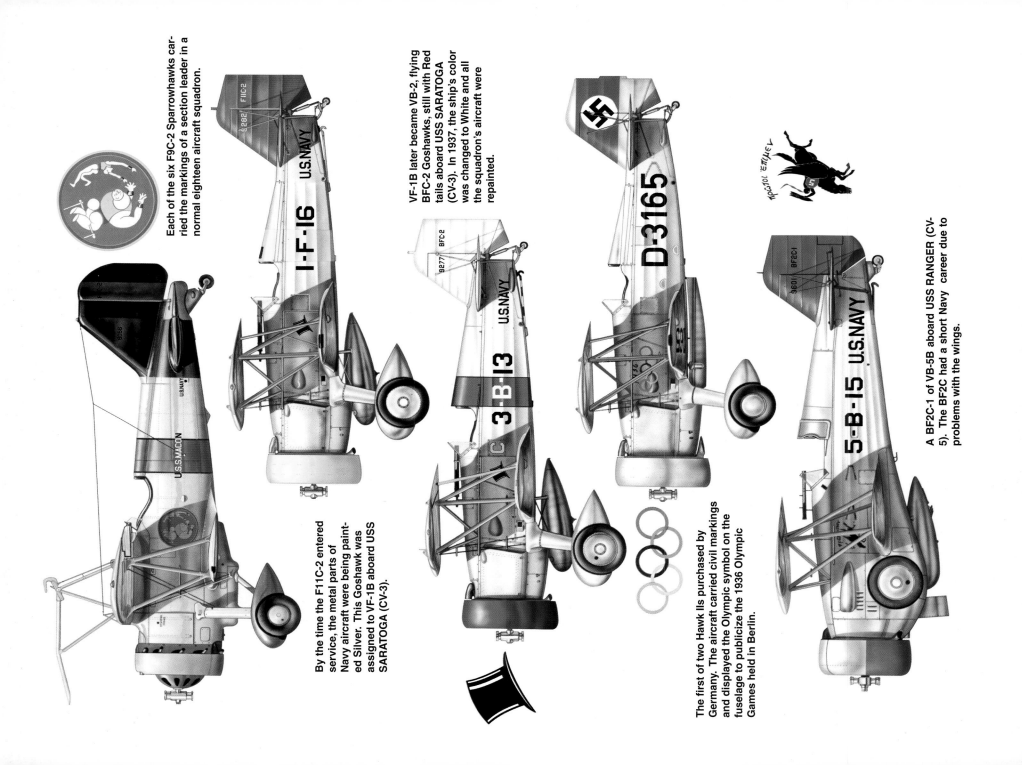

Each of the six F9C-2 Sparrowhawks carried the markings of a section leader in a normal eighteen aircraft squadron.

By the time the F11C-2 entered service, the metal parts of Navy aircraft were being painted Silver. This Goshawk was assigned to VF-1B aboard USS SARATOGA (CV-3).

VF-1B later became VB-2, flying BFC-2 Goshawks, still with Red tails aboard USS SARATOGA (CV-3). In 1937, the ship's color was changed to White and all the squadron's aircraft were repainted.

The first of two Hawk IIs purchased by Germany. The aircraft carried civil markings and displayed the Olympic symbol on the fuselage to publicize the 1936 Olympic Games held in Berlin.

A BF2C-1 of VB-5B aboard USS RANGER (CV-5). The BF2C had a short Navy career due to problems with the wings.

U.S.S.MACON

I-F-I6 U.S.NAVY

C-3-B-I3 U.S.NAVY

D-3165

5-B-I5 U.S.NAVY

F9C Sparrowhawk

The F9C Sparrowhawk (Curtiss Model 58) was a Navy fighter that was unsuccessful at the mission for which it was designed, but achieved success in another field that gave it fame all out of proportion to its performance and numbers.

In 1928 and 1929 the Navy's Bureau of Aeronautics laid out several new designs - Models 92 through 96 - for a new series of smaller shipboard fighters. All were biplanes with the upper wing attached directly to the top of the fuselage instead of being raised above the fuselage on struts. Because of the later use of the Sparrowhawk, for airship hook-on operations, it was widely believed that this design feature was added to the BuAir models with the pilot's forward and upward visibility, so essential to airship operations, in mind. In actuality, this was not the case and this type of wing design was part of the original concept.

Two manufacturers built directly-competing Navy-funded prototypes to meet the BuAir Model 96 requirements, Curtiss with the XF9C-l and General (formerly Atlantic and Fokker) with the XFA-l (A for Atlantic). Both were ordered in June of 1930, and had consecutive BuNos.

XF9C-1

The XF9C-1 (ordered as BuNo A-8731 but delivered as BuNo 873l because the Navy had dropped use of the A-prefix) was a big leap into the age of new construction technology for Curtiss. It featured all-metal construction, with a semi-monocoque aluminum fuselage. The

The XF9C-1 in its original configuration with a carrier deck arrester hook but no airship hook-on equipment. The Yellow coloring on top of the non-adjustable horizontal stabilizer extends to the top of the root fillet. (Curtiss)

The XF9C-1 had an under-fuselage support structure for the flying wires and inner landing gear struts, a forged Curtiss-Reid propeller, and individual exhaust stacks that were turned 180 degrees. (Curtiss 6625)

The XF9C-1 on the ramp at the Naval Aircraft Factory after being modified with a Wright R-975E engine with a forward exhaust collector manifold. The aircraft was fitted with a ground-adjustable two blade Hamilton-Standard propeller. (USN)

After being fitted with production F9C-2 landing gear, the XF9C-1 retained its front-side exhaust manifold when used as a spare plane for USS AKRON. The distinctive cartoon insignia of a fat and a thin trapeze artist was originated by Lieutenant Harrigan, one of the Sparrowhawk pilots. (Fred Bamberger)

tail surfaces were metal covered, while the wings and ailerons were fabric covered. Because of the aircraft's small size and the closeness of the wings, a sub-structure was built below the fuselage as an anchoring point for the flying wires. It also doubled as an anchor for the inner struts of the tripod landing gear.

Although the Navy had expressed preference for the new 400 hp Pratt & Whitney R-985 Wasp Jr air-cooled radial engine for the Model 96, Curtiss remained loyal to its Curtiss-Wright affiliation and fitted the aircraft with a Wright R-975C (J-6-9) nine-cylinder air cooled radial that delivered 400 hp at 2,300 rpm at sea level. The XF9C-l was the first Curtiss aircraft to have a Townend ring designed into it instead of being added later as a post-production modification.

The Wright J-6 series engines had their exhaust ports on the forward side of the cylinders, and these fed into a collector ring at the front of the crankcase. For the initial engine installation on the XF9C-l and the production F9C-2s, the exhaust system was changed to individual exhaust stacks which were turned 180 degrees to discharge behind the cylinders. The crankcase of the XF9C-1s was fitted with a large face plate having variable opening louvers for crankcase cooling. Later in its career, the XF9C-1 was re-engined with a 420 hp Wright R-975E engine with a front collector ring and a single large downward-pointing exhaust stack.

Since the exterior of the XF9C-l was mostly metal, it conformed to contemporary Navy painting standards in having all the metal surfaces painted in Light Gray (almost an Off-White color). Fabric areas were Silver, while the top of the upper wing and horizontal tail surfaces were Chrome Yellow.

The XF9C-l was built at Garden City, where it made its first flight on 12 February 1931. Equipped for carrier operations, it was tested by the Navy for that purpose, as was the competing XFA-1. The Pratt & Whitney Wasp powered Beliner-Joyce XFJ-l, while not directly competitive with the Curtiss and General designs, had been rejected earlier. As it turned out, th Navy quickly realized that the small carrier based biplane fighter concept just didn't work.

The Sparrowhawk was saved; however, when it was found that its small size suited it for use with the Navy's two new rigid airships, the USS AKRON (ZRS-4) and the USS MACON (ZRS-5). The Z in their designations identified them as being an airship rather than an airplane, the R identified them as rigid airships (not blimps), and the S indicated that they were to serve as scouts. The dash number identified the sequence of the Navy's rigid airships.

These airships were designed to carry aircraft and four Sparrowhawks could fit into the hangar bay in the belly of the ship while a fifth could be carried on an external station called, "The Perch."

With this new mission in mind, the XF9C-l was sent to the Naval Aircraft Factory for the installation of a Navy-designed aerial hook-on gear that had been developed earlier on a Vought UO-l biplane for hook-on tests with the older airship USS LOS ANGELES (ZR-3). The XF9C-l made its first hook-on to USS LOS ANGELES on 17 October 1931.

The cost of the XF9C-l complete was $74,442. It was assigned as a spare aircraft for USS AKRON, and then to USS MACON, all the while keeping its X-designation. At first, it retained its original 30 x 5.00 high-pressure wheels without wheel pants, but was later modified to use the smaller, low-pressure wheels and open-sided wheel pants of the F9C-2s.

After brief hook-on tests with USS MACON in the Summer of 1933, the XF9C-l was transferred to the Naval Aircraft Factory, where its hook was removed. It was then used for test and utility work. It was scrapped in January of 1935, with a total Navy flight time of only 213 hours.

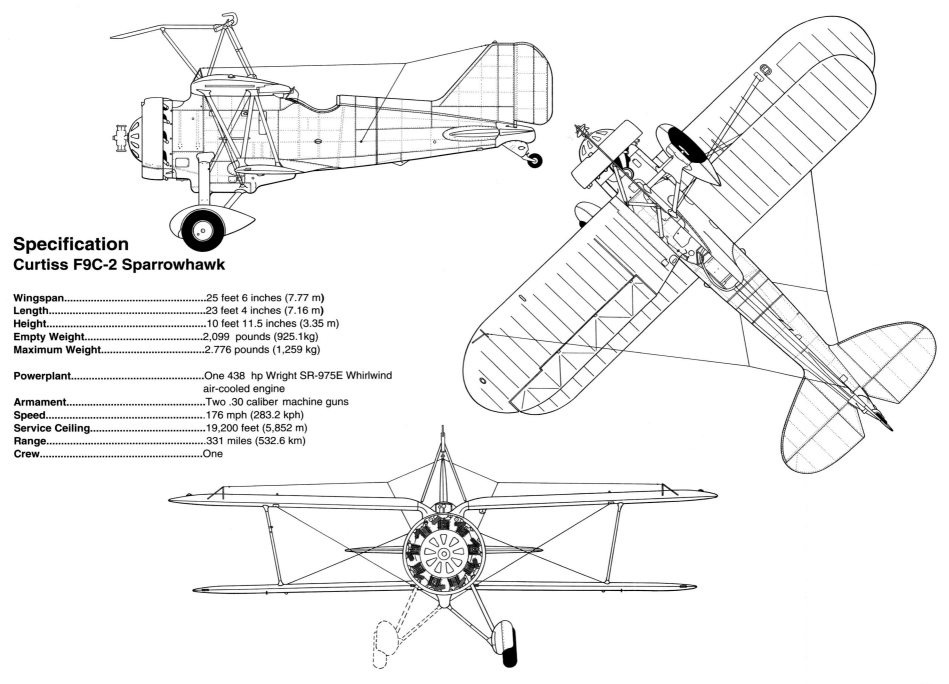

Specification
Curtiss F9C-2 Sparrowhawk

Wingspan...25 feet 6 inches (7.77 m)
Length..23 feet 4 inches (7.16 m)
Height...10 feet 11.5 inches (3.35 m)
Empty Weight...2,099 pounds (925.1kg)
Maximum Weight.....................................2.776 pounds (1,259 kg)

Powerplant...One 438 hp Wright SR-975E Whirlwind
air-cooled engine
Armament..Two .30 caliber machine guns
Speed...176 mph (283.2 kph)
Service Ceiling...19,200 feet (5,852 m)
Range...331 miles (532.6 km)
Crew...One

XF9C-2

During Navy evaluations of the XF9C-l, Curtiss built a second Sparrowhawk prototype as a company-funded project (Model 58A). This was unofficially called the XF9C-2 and carried the civil registration X986M. It was started at the Garden City plant, but since Curtiss-Wright was closing that plant as a depression economy, the project was moved to the new Kenmore plant near the main Curtiss plant in Buffalo. This had been built for Curtiss engine production, but since all engine work was transferred to Wright following the Curtiss-Wright merger of l929, the building became available for aircraft production. All subsequent Curtiss Hawk biplanes were built in the Kenmore plant.

The XF9C-2 differed from the XF9C-1 in a number of ways. To improve the pilot's visibility forward during such nose-high operations as landing, the upper wing was raised four inches to allow him to see under it. This resulted in a distinctive gull wing configuration. The fuselage itself remained essentially the same as the XF9C-1, and the rudder, originally balanced as on the XF9C-l, was enlarged and had the balance area deleted. The engine was a civil Wright R-975E, installed two inches lower in the fuselage to improve the pilot's forward visibility and make more room for the two .30 caliber machine guns.

The landing gear was a single-leg design similar to the XF6C-6. Later, this was changed to a rigid single-leg type with wire bracing and the shock absorbers built into the wheel pants. Although the Sparrowhawk had been rejected as a carrier-based fighter aircraft, the XF9C-2 was fitted with an arrester hook since operations at sea with the airships would likely require landings aboard a carrier.

As a privately owned airplane, the XF9C-2 prototype's coloring was not Navy standard. The fuselage, engine cowl, landing gear and struts were Command Blue or Admiral Blue which was used on aircraft assigned to Navy Flag Officers. The fabric was Silver except for the tops of the upper wing and horizontal tail, which were Chrome Yellow.

Based on tests of the XF9C-2, the Navy ordered six production F9C-2s that incorporated many of the improvements of the prototype XF9C-2. Curtiss made further changes to the

The XF9C-2 on the grass at NAS Anacostia while under going flight tests in November of 1931. The upper wing was some four inches higher position than the XF9C-1, the rudder was changed to a larger unbalanced type rudder, a X-prefix was added to the civil registration number, and there were two blast tubes installed for the two machine guns under the top of the Townend ring. (USN)

XF9C-2 as a result of Navy tests. The Navy finally bought the prototype in November of 1932, assigning it BuNo 9264. Brought up to production standards, including tripod landing gear and a still larger vertical tail, the XF9C-2 became a spare aircraft for both USS AKRON and USS MACON until the loss of USS MACON. Stripped of its hooks, it went on to serve as a utility aircraft until it was damaged in a forced landing in November of 1936. It was then broken up for spare parts to keep the surviving F9C-2s operational.

For a prototype aircraft, it was cheap. The Navy paid Curtiss only $29,253 for it and it ended its Navy career with a total flight time of 254 hours.

Modified to production F9C-2 standards with a revised vertical tail and new landing gear, the XF9C-2 under went a number of hook-on tests with USS MACON, including this test on 7 July 1933. As the spare Sparrowhawk for USS MACON, it did not carry unit markings. (USN)

The Curtiss-owned XF9C-2 prototype retained the balanced XF9C-1 style rudder. It carried a civil registration (986M) and had a straight single-leg landing gear with smaller-diameter low-pressure wheels in fully enclosed wheel pants. (Curtiss W-6894)

F9C-2

The Navy ordered six production F9C-2s (BuNos 9056/9061) during October of 1931. These incorporated most of the improvements made to the XF9C-2, including the installation of a 430 hp SR-975E radial engine. Only the first aircraft, BuNo 9056, was equipped with wire-braced single-leg landing gear. BuNo 9056's first flight, without airship hook-on gear, was on 14 April 1932. Deliveries of the other five were held up deliberately until the Navy completed further testing of BuNo 9056. The first change ordered was to remove the single leg landing gear and replace it with the tripod type landing gear used on the XF9C-1. Early flight tests of BuNo 9056 with the airship hook equipment installed revealed serious directional stability problems. These were corrected by adding a three-inch metal strip to the trailing edge of the rudder, this was only a temporary fix and the final solution to the problem was achieved by moving the rudder post to the rear, first by six inches and then by nine inches. This increased rudder leverage and added more side area to the vertical fin.

The remaining F9C-2s, with enlarged vertical tails, XF9C-1 landing gear and airship hooks attached, were delivered in August and September of 1932. Curtiss billed the Navy for each of the F9C-2s separately. BuNo 9056 was billed at $27,356 exclusive of GFE. The price for BuNo 9057 was $24,956, while BuNos 9058/9061 were $23,551 apiece. The Navy paid Wright $4,050 for each R-975E-3 engine.

The six F9C-2s and the two XF9Cs were to be divided between the USS AKRON and USS MACON, four Sparrowhawks to each airship. Following the loss of USS AKRON on 4 April 1933, fortunately with no Sparrowhawks aboard, all were transferred to USS MACON, which had been commissioned on 23 June 1933. All were sent with it to its new base at NAS Moffatt Field, near San Francisco, California.

The first F9C-2 was tested at NAS Hampton Roads, Virginia during June of 1932 with the airship hook installed. The ground-adjustable tab is visible on trailing edge of the rudder. The aircraft was equipped with XF9C-1 style landing gear, with small wheels and open-sided wheel pants. (USN)

This F9C-2 (BuNo 9057) assigned to USS MACON carries rudder stripes and the markings of a section leader in a standard eighteen aircraft Navy squadron. The fuselage band, wing chevrons, engine cowl, and wheel pants are White, the color of the second section. (USN)

The first production F9C-2 (BuNo 9056) during an early flight configured with the original single-strut landing gear and small tail. The tail lettering uses non-standard curved figures instead of the standard Navy block figures. (Curtiss)

became systematic. The aircraft flew out on headings 60 degrees from the airship's course. After flying for a specified time or distance, they turned inward 120 degrees on a course that would intercept the airship.

For some of these search missions, the Sparrowhawks did not take off independently of the airship as they usually did to make it "light" for takeoff. They were taken aloft with it, and then mechanics aboard the airship removed their landing gear, while in flight. Range was extended by installing a thirty gallon streamlined belly tank. Of course, the wheel-less aircraft had to return to the airship for recovery. Normally, they were kept aboard when the airship landed to add weight and reduce the need to valve expensive helium gas during the landing.

The Sparrowhawks were not part of a regular Navy squadron; they were auxiliaries of the airship. Each of the six F9C-2s had the status and markings of a section leader in a normal eighteen aircraft Navy squadron. The two X-models were spares and did not carry unit markings. When attached to USS AKRON, the F9C-2s carried vertical tail stripes. These deviated from Navy standard in that the forward (Blue) stripe was on the vertical fin rather than on the rudder. Shortly after transfer to USS MACON, the stripes were eliminated in favor of a unit color, all-Black tail surfaces.

The Sparrowhawks did not qualify for landings aboard aircraft carriers until December of 1933, when a problem arose. The smaller wheels of the F9C-2s had their hubs even with the cross-deck arresting wires. If a tire were to be deflected significantly, or even go flat, the wire would be above the wheel and its fairing and would snag the struts. The Navy recommended that the F9C-2s be fitted with the old 30 x 5.00 high-pressure wheels that would ride over the wires, but the Sparrowhawk pilots came up with a quick and easy fix. Small fin-like projections were built onto the fronts of the wheel pants to deflect the cross wires under the wheels when necessary.

When USS MACON crashed into the Pacific on 12 February 1935, four Sparrowhawks (BuNos 9058/9061), went down with her, The XF9C-2 and the two surviving F9C-2s (BuNos 9056, 9057) were then stripped of their hooks, redesignated as XF9C-2s, and assigned to limited utility roles. The last F9C-2 (BuNo 9056) was retired on 20 October 1939 with a total of 676.3 Navy flight hours. It was later rebuilt with parts of the second prototype, the original XF9C-2 (BuNo 9264). The Naval Aircraft Factory built a new hook for it, and it was put on display in the Smithsonian Institution in very inaccurate markings. It was withdrawn from

Three F9C-2 Sparrowhawks from USS MACON, (front to back) BuNo's 9059, 9056 and 9057. Each aircraft carries the fuselage band of a section leader, and the engine cowlings, wing chevrons and wheel pants are painted in section colors. (USN)

Sparrowhawks And Airships

The basing of aircraft on an airship was an operation unique in the world's military air services. As soon as the Sparrowhawks appeared, with their airship hooks, they immediately caught the fancy of the public and were promptly nicknamed "Akron Fighters." They were particularly popular with model builders, and several well-known model manufacturers quickly put kits on the market. Some were quite accurate while others were way off.

While the original idea of basing fighters on an airship may have intended them as defenders of the airship, that concept did not work. On various fleet maneuvers in which the airship itself was the scout, it was ruled "Shot down" by the referees. As a result, tactics soon changed. The airship did not venture into areas where it could be sighted by the enemy fleet; it stayed in safe territory and sent its aircraft out on scouting missions. Ultimately, this

The second production F9C-2 (BuNo 9057) flying from USS MACON with its landing gear replaced by a thirty gallon auxiliary fuel tank. This was a common practice to extend the range of the F9C-2s. (Paul Matt)

Two F9C-2s (BuNo 9058 and 9056) were used to qualify the Sparrowhawk for carrier operations. These aircraft conducted deck trials aboard USS LEXINGTON on 8 December 1933. (USN via F.H. Dean)

exhibit in 1959 and put in storage until 1971. It was then removed for refurbishment, painted accurately with its early USS MACON-era markings, and again put on exhibition for the 4 July 1976 opening of the new National Air & Space Museum in Washington, D.C.

This Sparrowhawk is the sole survivor of the 158 U.S. Navy Curtiss Hawk biplanes. Three others, a F6C-l, a F6C-4 and a BFC-2, are actually highly accurate full-scale reproductions.

USS MACON's No. 1 Sparrowhawk (BuNo 9056, section color Red) about to hook on to the airship's trapeze, which was known as the "Perch." The Townend ring carried the section color and the tail color, Black, extends over the rear fuselage. (USN)

A Sparrowhawk from USS MACON's Blue section on 8 February 1935. The aircraft has the section color on the fuselage, wing chevrons, and engine crankcase cover. It was fitted with prominent deflector vanes on wheel pants developed during deck trials on USS LEXINGTON. Also the Black tail color no longer covers the rear fuselage. Four days after this photographic flight, this aircraft was lost at sea with USS MACON. (USN)

The first F9C-2 (BuNo 9056) was restored and painted in early USS MACON markings for display in the National Air & Space Museum. It is not only the sole surviving Sparrowhawk, but is also the sole survivor of all 157 Curtiss Navy Hawks built between 1925 and 1935. (F.H. Dean)

33

F11C Goshawk

After the F7C-1 contract, Curtiss sold no more single-seat fighters to the Navy in squadron strength until l932. During this period, Boeing had become the sole supplier of Navy single-seaters with its new F4B series, twenty-seven F4B-l s, forty-six F4B-2s, twenty-one F4B-3s and ninety-two F4B-4s being delivered between mid-l928 and February of 1933.

This did not mean that Curtiss was out of favor with the Navy. During that same period it sold twenty-five two-seat F8C-l and F8C-3 fighters that were redesignated as OC-ls and OC-2s, and twenty-five notably different F8C-4s that were named the Helldiver. These were followed by sixty-three F8C-5s that were delivered without arresting gear and were soon redesignated as O2C-1s. These were augmented by another thirty aircraft built as O2C-ls. Curtiss also sold fifty-one N2C Fledgling primary trainers, thirty-one N2C-ls and twenty N2C-2s, to the Navy during the same period. Curtiss was obviously not hurting for Navy business.

The basic taper-winged Hawk biplane fighter made a comeback as the F11C Goshawk. Since Curtiss had advanced to all-metal construction with the F9C Sparrowhawk and some contemporary U.S. Army models, revival of the basic 1924 design was actually a step backward.

XF11C-1

While retaining the outlines of the old F6C-4, the new Goshawk that the Navy ordered in

The XF11C-1 Goshawk (BuNo 9217) was a return to the original F6C Hawk configuration of 1925 with many state-of-the-art upgrades. It featured a single-leg landing gear, cowled engine, and steerable tail wheel with hydraulic shock absorber. The BuNo and model designation had not yet been painted on the tall. (Curtiss W-7775 via F. H. Dean)

The XF11C-1 (in foreground) and a production F11C-2 in flight on 9 November 1932. The XF11C-1 differed from the production aircraft in the landing gear and engine installation. (Curtiss C-7863 via F.H. Dean)

April of l932, as the XF11C-l (BuNo 9217, Curtiss Model 64), was much more than an F6C-4 with a larger radial engine. It incorporated many modern features. The wings, still with the Clark Y airfoil, were now metal frames instead of wood. The ailerons and all tail surfaces were metal frames with metal skin, and the upper wing was raised three inches higher above the fuselage.

The engine was the new experimental Wright SR-1510, a fourteen cylinder twin-row, air-cooled radial, that delivered 600 hp at 2,100 rpm at 8,000 feet. Covered by a full NACA cowling, it drove a three-blade, eight foot six inch diameter propeller. The smaller diameter

Early modifications to the XF11C-1 included lengthening the landing gear and installing a larger-diameter two-blade propeller. The aircraft now carries the type code (XF11C-2) and BuNo on the tail. (Curtiss)

The XF11C-1 on the ramp at the Curtiss Buffalo, N.Y. facility on 25 September 1933. Factory testing of the XF11C-1 continued for nearly a year and included tests with a longer-chord cowling. (Curtiss W-8547 via F .H. Dean)

allowed the use of a shorter-than-normal landing gear. The wheels were the standard Navy 30 x 5.00 high-pressure type in open-sided wheel pants. A new steerable tail wheel was installed at the extreme rear fuselage and required a cut-out in the bottom of the rudder to accommodate the hydraulic shock absorber. All metal parts were painted Light Gray except the tops of the ailerons and horizontal tail. A11 fabric areas except the top of the upper wing, which was Chrome Yellow, were Silver.

During 1934, the XF11C-1 was redesignted as the XBFC-1 fighter-bomber and loaned to the NACA for engine cowling and cooling tests. The aircraft was outfitted with a cooling fan in the cowl throat and had the cowling faired into the flat-sided fuselage to improve airflow. The aircraft was also fitted with test instrumentation on a boom mounted on the starboard outer wing strut. (NACA)

The first flight was in October of l932. The R-1510 engine proved to be unsatisfactory due to overheating, so various cowling arrangements were tried to overcome the cooling problems. The propeller was changed to a nine foot ten inch diameter two blade unit and to maintain the required ground clearance, the landing gear legs were lengthened. This also gave the aircraft a higher ground angle and permitted a lower landing speed. The three-blade propeller was soon restored, but the higher landing gear was retained.

The XF11C-1 cost the Navy $65,306.68, including GFE. In March of 1934, it was given the new Bomber-fighter designation XBFC-1 and soon after was turned over to NACA for research into the cooling of tightly-cowled radial engines. The XBFC-1 was retired in March of 1939, with only 319.4 hours of Navy flying time.

XF11C-2

The XF11C-2 (BuNo 9213, Curtiss Model 64A) is a bit confusing, because it has a later designation than the XF11C-l, but was an older aircraft with a lower BuNo. The Navy contract for the XF11C-2, an off-the-shelf Curtiss Hawk II, also known as the Goshawk, was signed and the naval designation and BuNo assigned to it before the contract for the yet-to-be-built XF11C-l, which was already designated as such, was signed and its BuNo issued.

The XF11C-2 was an even longer backward step than was the XF11C-l. The wings were again wood frames and the tail surfaces were fabric covered. A narrow Townend ring covered the nine-cylinder single-row Wright SR-l820F Cyclone engine that delivered 600 hp at 1,950 rpm at 8000 feet. A two-blade propeller was used and a louvered face plate covered the front of the crankcase. The landing gear was notably longer than the final form of the XF11C-l and used smaller-diameter low-pressure wheels. The tail wheel was located farther forward than even on the F6C-l. Later, the XF11C-2, was modified to use the XF11C-l tail wheel form and location, with a cut-out at the bottom of the rudder.

The XF11C-2 (BuNo 9213) was an earlier airplane acquired by the Navy before the contract for the XF11C-1 was signed. Some of the differences were the longer landing gear legs and smaller-diameter low pressure tires, narrow Townend ring around a single-row Wright R-i820E Cyclone engine and underfuselage F6C type fuel tank. (Curtiss W-7243)

35

Fuselage Development

XF11C-1

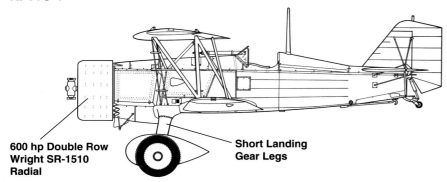

600 hp Double Row Wright SR-1510 Radial

Short Landing Gear Legs

F11C-2

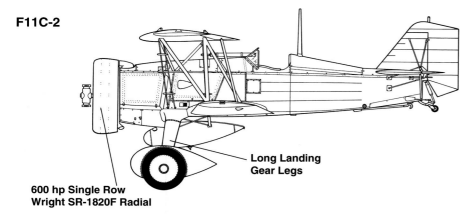

Long Landing Gear Legs

600 hp Single Row Wright SR-1820F Radial

Coloring for the XF11C-2 was the contemporary Navy standard of Silver for fabric areas, Light Gray for metal parts and Chrome Yellow for the top of the upper wing and horizontal tail. (Curtiss W-7244)

The XF11C-2 in flight with a 500 pound bomb installed on the underfuselage displacement gear. The engine has a louvered crankcase cover and the tail wheel is further forward on the underside of the fuselage than on the XF11C-1. (Curtiss C-7290)

The XF11C-2 was a true vertical dive bomber. To prevent the 500 pound centerline bomb from falling through the propeller during a vertical dive (actually at an aircraft angle of 95 degrees to achieve "Zero Lift" on the wings) the bomb rack, called Displacement Gear, swung away from the fuselage to place the bomb clear of the propeller arc. Smaller bombs could also be carried on under wing racks.

The XF11C-2 flew for the first time in March of 1932, and beat the XF11C-1 for a Navy contract for twenty-eight production F11C-2s. The XF11C-2 cost the Navy $42,530.00 including GFE. It crashed in August of 1932 with only 74 hours total flight time on the aircraft.

The XF11C-2 on the ramp at Naval Air Station Anacostia, Virginia, on 19 July 1932, while undergoing bombing tests with two 116 pound bombs on the underwing bomb racks . (USN)

Final configuration of the XF11C-2 with a XF11C-1 tail wheel installation located at end of fuselage with a cut-out in the rudder to accommodate the shock absorber. The aircraft is carrying a new streamlined fifty gallon auxiliary fuel tank on under fuselage bomb rack. (USN)

The first production F11C-2 (BuNo 9265) under test at Naval Air Station Hampton Roads, Virginia, in December of 1932. The tail lettering is in curved form, not the standard Navy block form. The flotation bag compartment was on the underside of the upper wing outboard of the interplane struts. (USN)

This F11C-2 has the underwing flotation bags deployed from their containers located on the underside of the upper wing outboard of the interplane struts. These bags were intended to keep the aircraft afloat long enough for it to be salvaged. (USN)

F11C-2

Delivery of the twenty-eight production F11C-2s (BuNos 9265/9282, 9331/9340) began in March of 1933. These were nearly identical to the final XF11C-2 configuration except for 30 x 5.00 wheels and deletion of the louvered crankcase cover. Initial fleet service was with the famous High Hat squadron , VF-1B, aboard USS SARATOGA. At that time the unit flew a mixed group of F11C-s and Boeing F4B-3s. There was no directly comparable new Boeing model ordered at the same time as the F11C-2s, but eighteen of the F11C-2s were ordered just ahead of the last thirty-eight of the eighty-two Boeing F4B-4s.

In spite of their increased weight, power and speed, the F11C-2s retained the same pleasant handling characteristics their lighter Hawk predecessors. The need for the pilot to hold offset right rudder during climb and cruise was eliminated after the Goshawks were in service by the addition of a small ground-adjustable sheet-metal tab to the trailing edge of the rudder.

The F11C-2s cost $13,000 each, apart from GFE and the Navy was paying $6,243.00 each for SR-l820F Cyclone engines.

BFC-2

Early in 1934, the F11C-2s were upgraded in the field with kits sent from the Curtiss factory. These modification kits added a new and higher rear turtledeck to the fuselage and a partial sliding canopy now enclosed the rear half of the open cockpit. This modification led to a change of designation to BFC-2. The 575 hp SR-1820F-2 engine had already been redesignated as the R-1820-78. As dual-purpose bomber/fighter aircraft, the BFC-2s operated at two different gross weights, with performance affected accordingly.

Initial deliveries of F11C-2s were to the Red-tailed VF-1B High Hat Squadron aboard USS SARATOGA. This is the No. 3 aircraft of the first section in the squadron and it carries the correct block form of tail lettering in White on the Red tail. (R.L. Cavanagh Collection)

Changing naval policies resulted in several squadron and marking changes for VF-1B and its F11C-2/BFC-2s during the High Hat's use of the Goshawk over a five-year period. This time is believed to be a record for a carrier squadron's use of the same aircraft type during the pre-Second World War years. First, VF-1B was redesignated VB-2B during 1934 while still serving aboard USS SARATOGA. In July of l937, the Navy changed the way it designated

For a brief period during 1933, VB-2B at Naval Air Station Moffett Field, Californis operated with a mix of new BFC-2s and older Boeing F4B-4s (left). The aircraft in the center are Grumman SF-1s. (Dave Lucabaugh Collectiom)

Fuselage Development

F11C-2

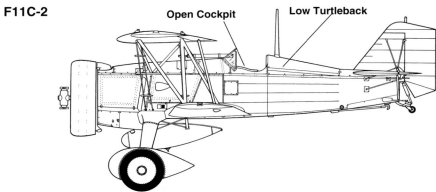

Open Cockpit   Low Turtleback

BFC-2

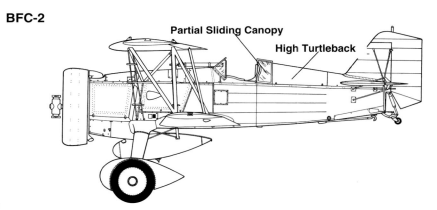

Partial Sliding Canopy

High Turtleback

the squadrons aboard aircraft carriers. All the squadrons on a particular ship now took the hull number of that ship as the squadron number. Squadrons aboard USS SARATOGA (CV-3) all became "threes." Accordingly, VB-2B became VB-3 for the bomber squadron; VF-6B, the fighter squadron, became VF-3, etc. The suffix letters designating the Battle and Scouting Forces were eliminated. The tail colors also changed. Each carrier group now had its own color, so the old VF-1B/VB-2B Red tail was changed to the White tail carried by all USS SARATOGA aircraft.

When VB-3's BFC-2s were replaced by two-seat Vought SB2U-1s, eleven of the Goshawks were assigned to the new Carrier Air Group that was then being formed for the new USS ENTERPRISE (CV-6) and joined Squadron VB-6 ,(formerly VB-8B), which was then flying Boeing F4B-4s. The BFC-2s were transferred to VB-6 during January and February of 1938, but few went aboard the ship when it was commissioned on 12 May 1938. Some were transferred out and others were damaged or scrapped. Three were surveyed on 10 June l938, for "general wear incident to service." Three others were removed from the ship during its shake-

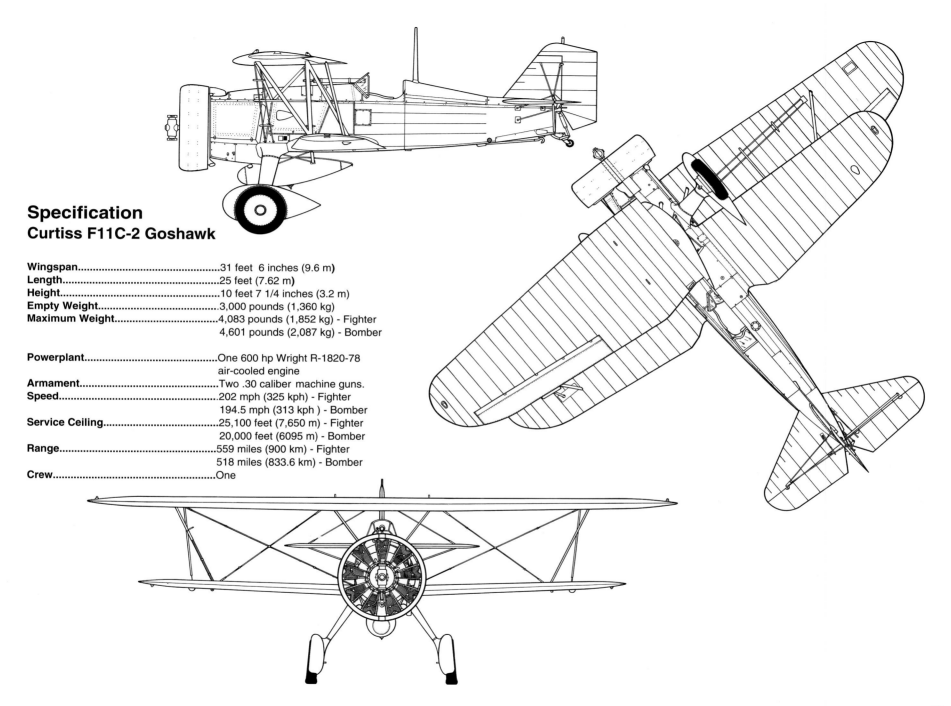

Specification
Curtiss F11C-2 Goshawk

Wingspan...31 feet 6 inches (9.6 m)
Length...25 feet (7.62 m)
Height...10 feet 7 1/4 inches (3.2 m)
Empty Weight...3,000 pounds (1,360 kg)
Maximum Weight...................................4,083 pounds (1,852 kg) - Fighter
                              4,601 pounds (2,087 kg) - Bomber

Powerplant..One 600 hp Wright R-1820-78
                              air-cooled engine
Armament..Two .30 caliber machine guns.
Speed...202 mph (325 kph) - Fighter
                              194.5 mph (313 kph) - Bomber
Service Ceiling......................................25,100 feet (7,650 m) - Fighter
                              20,000 feet (6095 m) - Bomber
Range...559 miles (900 km) - Fighter
                              518 miles (833.6 km) - Bomber
Crew...One

VF-1B was redesignated as Bomber-Fighter Squadron VB-2B and its F11C-2s were modified and redesignated as BFC-2s. The modifications included a higher rear turtledeck, partial sliding canopy (that covered only the rear of the cockpit) and camera gun mounted on upper wing center section. (E.M. Sommerich Collection)

down cruise to South America and were surveyed at Coco Solo, Panama.

There was no single "last BFC-2". In December of 1938, a directive from BuAir grounded all of the surviving BFC-2s because of their age and condition. The high time BFC-2 was BuNo 9332, with a total of 1,475.8 hours. Twelve other BFC-2 each exceeded 1,000 hours.

XF11C-3

The last modern feature added to the now venerable Hawk biplane was a retractable landing gear. The fifth production F11C-2 (BuNo 9269) was kept at the Curtiss factory for conversion to the XF11C-3 (Curtiss Model 67). It featured wheels that retracted flush into the modified lower nose. The retraction system was a chain drive, hand-cranked into position by the pilot. Grumman had developed this system on amphibious seaplane floats and first used it on a production aircraft with the two-seat FF-1 fighter of 1931 and followed that with the F2F-l single-seat fighter.

The modification added 230 pounds to the empty weight of the airframe, which used the same SR-1820F engine as the Fl1C-2. The added weight of the new landing gear ahead of the center of gravity required that the upper wing be moved slightly forward of its original F11C-2 position. First flight of the XF11C-3 took place during April of 1933, with the aircraft being delivered to the Navy on 27 May 1933.

The aircraft's normal gross weight was 4,419 pounds and overload gross weight was 4,803 pounds. The top speed was 216 mph at 8,000 feet with a two-blade fixed-pitch propeller. Later, the propeller was changed to variable-pitch, and the turtledeck was changed to that used on the BFC-2. In its final form the XF11C-3 also had pilot-controlled elevator trim tabs, in addition to the original adjustable stabilizer and inset controllable rudder tab. In March of 1934, the XF11C-3 was redesignated as the XBF2C-l Bomber-fighter.

On 24 September 1934, the XBF2C-1 experienced engine failure on takeoff from NAS Hampton Roads, Virginia and ditched in salt water. It was surveyed after accumulating 253

The High Hat squadron was redesignated again during 1937, when it became VB-3 based aboard USS SARATOGA (CV-3). With the change in designator came a change in tail color, this time to White. BuNo 9277, on the ramp at Griffith Park, California on 12 July 1937, has had the partial sliding canopy deleted. (B.C. Reed)

hours 45 minutes of Navy flight time.

BF2C-1

Testing of the XF11C-3 resulted in a production order for twenty-seven F11C-3s (BuNos 9686/9712, Curtiss Model 67A). These were all redesignated as BF2C-ls by the time the first one flew in September of 1934. The BF2C-1 was externally identical to the XF11C-3, but featured two major internal changes. The wings used the metal framework of the XF11C-l and the airfoil was changed to the NACA 2212. The engine was the R-1820-04 driving a controllable-pitch propeller and delivering 700 hp at 8,000 feet (when the R-1820 dash numbers reached l00, the Navy started a new series at -02). The cost of a BF2C-1, not including GFE, was $18,000.00. The Navy's cost for the Cyclone engine was now down to $5,749.00.

Competition for the new Curtiss was now provided by Grumman, not Boeing, which had gotten out of the biplane fighter business after delivering the last F4B-4. Grumman received an order for fifty-four F2F-ls right after the BF2C-l order was placed.

Delivery of BF2C-ls to Squadron VB-5B aboard the new carrier USS RANGER (CV-4) began in November of 1934. That Green-tailed squadron was the only one to use the BF2C-l, and in contrast to the F11C-2/ BFC-2, it had the shortest career in carrier squadron service of any single-seat Navy fighter.

As another dual-purpose Navy airplane, the BF2C-1 also operated at two gross weights. As a fighter it had an empty weight of 3,329 pounds and a gross weight of 4,555 pounds. Top speed was 225 mph at 8,000 feet and the service ceiling was 27,000 feet. As a bomber, empty weight was the same but the gross weight was 5,086 pounds. The top speed dropped to 215 mph and the service ceiling was lowered to 22,700 feet.

Fourteen BFC-2s of VB-2B parked inside the airship hangar at Naval Air Station Moffett Field, California just before the base was turned over to the Army after loss of the airship USS MACON. Aircraft 2-B-13 (section color Green) has the aircraft number 13 inside the wing chevron while 2-B-l5 next to it has no wing chevron or number. (Dave Lucabaugh Collection)

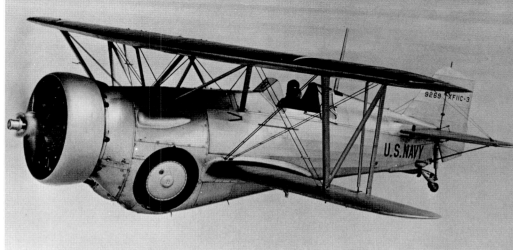

The XF11C-3 shared a number of features with the BFC-2 including the raised turtledeck and partial sliding canopy. (Curtiss W-8554 via F.H. Dean)

BF2C-1 Service Problems

Totally unforeseen problems limited the BF2C-1s career to a little over a year. While the metal-frame Hawk wings were satisfactory on the Army XP-23 and the Navy XF11C-1, those aircraft had different engines than the BF2C-1. The natural period of vibration of the metal wings harmonized with the vibrations of the Cyclone engine with the result that the aircraft

The XF11C-3 had a concave under fuselage section that partially enclosed the 500 pound bomb or under fuselage fuel tank. There are flotation bag compartments in the tips of the upper wing. (Curtiss)

Fuselage Development

BFC-2

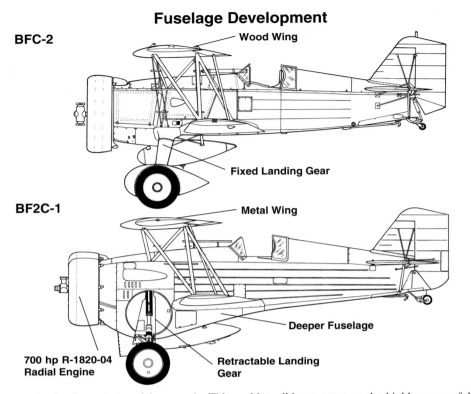

Wood Wing

Fixed Landing Gear

BF2C-1

Metal Wing

Deeper Fuselage

700 hp R-1820-04
Radial Engine

Retractable Landing Gear

The XF11C-3 after being it was redesignated as the XBFC-1 during 1934. The canopy was in the closed position and a half-round cowling has been added to the lower fuselage just ahead of auxiliary fuel tank to help eliminate tail buffeting. (Curtiss)

nearly shook apart at cruising speed. This problem did not occur on the highly successful Curtiss Hawk III, an export model that was identical to the BF2C-1, except for using wood-frame wings.

The Navy and Curtiss tried in many ways to eliminate or at least reduce this unacceptable condition. Weights were attached to the wingtips to change the wing harmonics, and for one test, the flying wires were rigged so tight that the metal interplane struts bowed. To see if some of the vibration was caused by air flow over the nose, a pusher propeller was installed on a water-cooled Curtiss V-1570 engine mounted on a test stand and the blast was directed over the BF2C-1 as though from its own propeller.

A test of wooden Hawk III wings on a BF2C-1 came too late to save the operational career of the BF2C-l; the cost of replacement wings for the entire BF2C-1 fleet could not be justified. A related problem was tail buffering caused by turbulent air-flow behind the 500 pound bomb or the auxiliary fuel tank and their associated attachments in the concave under fuselage section. This was partially relieved by the addition of a semi-circular cowling that formed a venturi to smooth out the airflow ahead of the bomb or fuel tank. The device had been tested on the XBF2C-l and was fitted to BF2C-ls after they were in service.

A weak landing gear was another of the BF2C-1s troubles. All of these problems led to a withdrawal of the BF2C-l from service with VB-5B between October of 1935 and February of 1936. They were replaced with old Boeing F4B-4s until the squadron could be re-equipped with new Grumman F3F-1s. The BF2C-l situation led to serious Navy correspondence on the

subject of Curtiss' suitability as a designer and builder of Naval aircraft.

Following their withdrawal from the fleet, Curtiss proposed a weight reduction program for the BF2C-l with a view to their being used as fighter-trainers at Pensacola. This idea was rejected. In January of 1937, a letter from the Secretary of the Navy directed that nineteen of the surviving BF2C-ls, not including two then being used in test programs, be grounded and scrapped because they were considered unfit for use due to excessive vibration. It is reported that those stationed in San Diego were stripped of their engines and other useful equipment, loaded on barges, and dumped at sea. A sorry finale to the one year career of the 132 taper-winged Navy Hawks.

The high-time BF2C-1 (BuNo 9601) had only 295 hours on it when. it was finally grounded.

This Green-tailed BF2C-1 (BuNo 9601) was assigned to USS ENTERPRISE (CV-6) has the canopy in the fully open position. The BF2C-1 had an inset rudder tab and mass balances added to the elevators in attempt to reduce tail flutter. (A.U. Schmidt Collection)

Section One of VB-5B flies in formation during March of 1935. The aircraft have been modified with venturi cowlings added ahead of underfuselage fuel tanks. Engine cowl coloring is correct for a full section; No. 1 full cowl, No. 2 top half of cowling, No. 3 bottom half of cowling. (USN)

A BF2C-1 of Bombing Five (VB-5) on the ramp at March Field, California. The aircraft is fitted with a bomb rack on the outboard wing panel of the lower wing and an external fuel tank on the underfuselage bomb rack. (Dave Lucabaugh Collection)

All eighteen BF2C-1s of VB-5B on parade in a double Vee formation of nine aircraft each. This illustrates the purpose of top-wing chevrons; it was a visual aid to allow each pilot to line up on the chevron of the aircraft ahead of him. (USN)

43

Civil And Export Hawks

A total of 301 taper-winged Hawk biplane fighters were built for other customers, compared to 238 for the U.S. Army and 132 for the U.S. Navy (not including the straight-wing F7C and F9C models). While all of these appear on the master list of Curtiss aircraft, not all are matched to the retroactive 1935 Curtiss model numbers.

Until 1930, the Curtiss export sales name matched the equivalent U.S. military model. From 1930 onward, all export aircraft were identified as Hawks followed by a Roman Numeral; i.e., P-6 airframes were Hawk Is and Hawk IAs, F11C-2 airframes were Hawk IIs, etc.

The biplane Hawks built as demonstrators carried U.S. civil registrations, which were canceled if the aircraft was sold abroad. One widely used demonstrator, the Doolittle Hawk, retained its original registration after finding a new American owner. Another Hawk, the Al Williams famous Gulfhawk, still has its 1930 registration and is currently on display in the U.S. Marine Aviation Museum at Quantico, Virginia.

By the time the Hawk II went on the market, the biplane Hawk was obsolescent by the standards of the world's major air forces, and it made no technical contributions to the subsequent designs of other nations. Although unknown at the time, one sale was to have a major effect on subsequent aviation history.

Ernst Udet, Germany's highest-scoring surviving First World War Ace (62 victories), one of the world's leading aerobatic pilots, and an aircraft designer, was greatly impressed by Al Williams' demonstrations of precision dive-bombing in the Gulfhawk I at the National Air Races. Udet then persuaded the German Air Ministry to purchase two Hawk IIs for the still-secret Luftwaffe to be used in the study and evaluation of vertical dive-bombing techniques. The result was the notorious Junkers Ju 87 Stuka and its widespread use by the Luftwaffe in the Second World War II.

The first German Hawk II was delivered early in 1934 with German civil registration D-3165. This was changed to D-IRIS when the German registration system was changed from numbers to letters later that year. The second was delivered as D-IRIK.

The export Hawk I for Japan was similar to the water-cooled U.S. Army P-6 Hawk modified with a larger chin radiator. While under test in the U.S., the aircraft carried the civil registration 72K on the rudder in Black. (Curtiss T-5562)

Civil And Export Curtiss Hawk Biplanes

Sales Name	Curtiss Model	Customer	Quantity	Year	Remarks
PW-8	33A	Japan	1	1924	Hawk Predecessor - not in totals
P-1	34A	Bolivia	4	1927	
	34G	Chile	8	1926	
	34G	Japan	1	1927	
P-1B	34I	Chile	8	1927	
Hawk I		Curtiss	1	1929	Doolittle Hawk (NR9110)
		Holland	8	1930	8 built in Holland
		Japan	1	1930	Japaneze Hawk**
Hawk IA		Cuba	3	1930	Cuban Hawk P-6 Wasp Engine
		Gulf Oil	1	1939	Gulfhawk I (NR982V)
Hawk II		Bolivia	9	1932-33	Used in combat.
		Chile*	4	1935	
		China	50	1933	Used in combat
		Colombia	26	1932-34	Land and Sea
		Cuba	4	1933	
		Germany	2	1933	Dive Bombers
		Norway	1	1934	ex-X13263 Demonstrator
		Siam (Thailand)	12	1934	Used in combat
		Turkey	19	1932	Turkey Hawk
Hawk III	68	Argentina	10	1936	
	68C	China	102	1936-38	Used in combat
	68A	Civil	1	1934	Demonstrator
	68B	Siam (Thailand)	24	1935-36	Used in combat
		Turkey	1	1935	Turkey Demonstrator (NR16Y)
Hawk IV		Argentina	1	1936	Demonstrator (NR188M)

*There is reason to believe that these aircraft may have actually been delivered to Peru for service in its war against Colombia. It is known that three Sea Hawk IIs and one land Hawk II were used by Peru, although no Curtiss records reveal a contract or delivery date.
**When Curtiss released photographs of the export Japanese Hawk, they mis-spelled the name and called the aircraft the Japaneze Hawk.

The eight Hawk Is for Holland were also export versions of the water-cooled P-6. H-1 was overall Khaki Brown except for the top of upper wing and horizontal tail, which were chrome yellow. Eight additional examples were built under license in Holland. (Thijs Postma)

Export versions of the U.S. Navy F11C-2 were marketed as the Curtiss Hawk II, also known as the Goshawk. This was one of nineteen built for Turkey during 1932. Curtiss captioned the photo "Turkey Hawk" and the name stuck. The flush-fitting under fuselage jettisonable detachable belly tank is different than that used on the Navy the F11C-2. In service the Turkish Hawks were camouflaged in overall Dark Brown. (Curtiss 7617)

Len Povey, an American who commanded the Cuban air Force, poses beside the Cuban Hawk II that he was flying when he originated the "Cuban Eight" maneuver at the 1936 Miami air Races. This maneuver has been a standard with air show pilots ever since. (Joe Christy)

Ernst Udet, Germany's highest-scoring surviving First World War Ace (62 victories) was greatly impressed by Al Williams' dive-bombing demonstrations in the Gulfhawk I at the National Air Races. He persuaded the German Air Ministry to purchase two Hawk IIs to be used in the study and evaluation of vertical dive-bombing techniques. This aircraft also carried a flush-fitting under fusealge fuel tank. (Curtiss)

The Hawk IIs sold to Colombia between 1932 and 1934 could be flown either as land-planes or as float seaplanes. When on floats, the Hawk IIs had a small fin installed below the fuselage which was necessary to maintain directional stability when operating on floats. The pilot of this Hawk II (Sea) has left the water rudders in the down position. (Curtiss via F.H. Dean)

Combat

Several export Hawk biplane fighters saw combat in a number of countries. Hawk IIs saw combat in Bolivia, China and Siam (Thailand). In Bolivia they saw action during the Gran Chaco War against Paraguay. The Bolivian Hawk IIs were outfitted with underwing bomb racks and used mainly for tactical reconnaissance and ground support. There were; however, several instances of air-to-air combat and several kills were credited to the Hawk IIs. By the time the war ended, the Bolivian Hawk II force had been reduced to three airworthy fighters.

Peru used at least three float equipped Hawk IIs against Colombia. These aircraft operated from Iquitos on the Amazon River.

In China, the Chinese Air Force Order of Battle in July of 1937, included both the Hawk II and Hawk III. Hawk IIs equipped the 21st, 22nd and 23rd Pursuit Squadrons, 4th Group based at Nan-Chang Air Base, the 7th Pursuit Squadron, 3rd Group at Chu-Jung Air Base, and the 24th, 25th and 28th Pursuit Squadrons, 5th Group at Nan-Chang Air Base. Hawk IIIs

A flight of Colombian Hawk II (Sea) fighters. Colombia was the largest Hawk II user in Latin America, receiving a total of twenty-six aircraft between July of 1932 and July of 1934. The aircraft were flown both as land and sea based fighters, flying from Colombia's many rivers. In August of 1944, some thirteen still remained in service, and the last report of active Hawk IIs was in August of 1946, when five were reported as being in use as liaison aircraft. (H. J. Nowarra)

equipped the 5th Reconnaissance Squadron, 6th Group at Nanking Air Base, and the 6th, 12th and 16th Reconnaissance Squadrons, 7th Group at Sian Air Base. These units fought both defensive and offensive missions against the Japanese around Shanghai, scoring some success against Japanese bomber formations. With the introduction of the A5M fighter, the Japanese quickly gained air superiority over the Chinese biplane fighter force. As they were replaced by Soviet supplied I-15/152 and I-153 fighters, the surviving Hawks were transferred to the advanced training role.

Four Siamese (Thai) fighter squadrons were equipped with Hawk IIIs and one was operating Hawk IIs during late 1940 when France and Siam engaged in a short border war. The Hawks flew escort, interception and dive-bombing missions against French forces based in Indochina. The survivors of these fighters again saw action on 7 December 1941, when Japanese forces invaded Thailand. This action was short-lived as peace talks led to a cease fire later that day. One Hawk III remains preserved in Thailand as part of the Thai Air Force Museum at Don Muang Air Base, near Bangkok.

(Above & Right) Four Siamese (Thai) fighter squadrons were equipped with Hawk IIIs during late 1940 when France and Siam engaged in a short border war. The Hawks flew escort, interception and dive-bombing missions against French forces based in Indochina. Later these fighters again saw action on 7 December 1941, when Japanese forces invaded Thailand. One Hawk III remains preserved in Thailand as part of the Thai Air Force Museum at Don Muang Air Base, near Bangkok. Shortly after they were delivered, Thai Hawk IIIs were camouflaged with two tone Brown and Green uppersurfaces over Light Blue undersurfaces. During the fighting with France, the Hawks carried a representation of the Thai flag on the wings. After the Japanese occupation, the Hawks carried the Running Elephant insignia, which was used until 1945. The blister on the fuselage side covers the machine gun breech and the cowling throat is notched to allow clearance for the guns. (Curtiss)

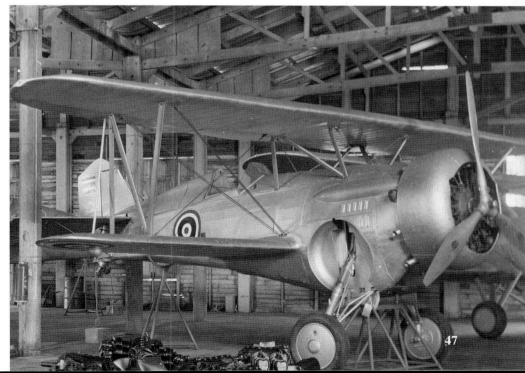

One of the 102 Hawk IIIs delivered to China on the dirt ramp of a Chinese air base during 1944. By this time the Hawks were used as advanced trainers. Aircraft 88 was overall Dark Brown with White numbers and Blue and White rudder stripes. The aircraft was modified with a three blade propeller and, contrary to some reports, none of the Hawk IIIs were build from scratch in China, although many were assembled from kits provided by Curtiss. Chinese Hawk IIIs carried the national insignia on the top of the upper wing and underside of the lower wing. This aircraft has the fuselage gun blisters deleted.

The last model in the long line of Hawk biplanes was the single Hawk IV, built during 1935 and sold to Argentina, where it served alongside ten Hawk IIIs. It differed from the Hawk III in having a raised turtledeck and fully enclosed canopy. Hawk III deliveries continued into 1938. (Curtiss SF-9812)

Curtiss Factory Designations for U.S. Military Hawks

Curtiss Model	Military Designation	Using Service	Quantity	Remarks
34	XPW-8A	Army	1	Became XPW-8 and P-1 Prototype
34A	P-1	Army	25	1st A/C became XP-17 Last five became P-2s
34B	P-2	Army	5	Last five P-1s, one became the XP-6
34C	F6C-1	Navy	9	First a/c became the F6C-4 and XF6C-5. Last 4 became F6C-2s
34D	F6C-2	Navy	4	Last four F6C-1s
34E	F6C-3	Navy	35	One became the F6C-6 racer and later became the XF6C-6 monoplane
34G	P-1A	Army	25	Plus 3 ex-P-2s. One each used for XP-6A, XAT-4A, XP-3A, and XP-22
34H	F6C-4	Navy	31	One temporarily designated as XF6C-7
34I	P-1B	Army	25	
34J	XAT-4	Army	1	ex-P-1A
	AT-4	Army	40	Thirty-five became P-6Ds, five became AT-5s
34K	AT-5	Army	5	Last 5 AT-4s. All later became P-1Es
34L	P-5	Army	5	P-1A airframes with turbosuperchargers
34M	XAT-5	Army	31	All became P-1Fs
34N	XP-3A	Army	2	One ex-P-1A, one ex-P-3A. Both converted to XP-21s
34O	P-3A	Army	5	One became second XP-3A, 1929 racer. Later converted to XP-21
	P-1C	Army	33	Last converted to XP-6E
34P	XP-6	Army	1	ex-P-2
	P-6/P-6A	Army	18	nine each and 2 P-6As from unfinished P-11 airframes. All converted to P-6Ds
34Q	XP-6A	Army	1	ex-P-1A, 1927 racer
35	YP-20	Army	1	3rd P-11 airframe, converted to XP-6E and later XP-6F
	P-6E	Army	46	One each converted to XP-6G, XP-6H, and XP-23
35C	XP-6F	Army	1	ex-XP-6E (YP-20)
43	XF7C-1	Navy	1	Delivered as production a/c
	F7C-1	Navy	17	Most to USMC
58	XF9C-1	Navy	1	Airship fighter
58A	XF9C-2	Navy	1	Improved XF9C-1
	F9C-2	Navy	6	Four lost with USS MACON
63	XP-23	Army	1	Redesign of last P-6E, converted to YP-23
64	XF11C-1	Navy	1	Major upgrade of F6C-4 Converted to XBFC
64A	XF11C-2	Navy	1	Off-the-shelf Hawk I
	F11C-2	Navy	28	Later redesignated BFC-2
67	XF11C-3	Navy	1	Fifth F11C-2 rebuilt with retractable landing gear, redesignated as XBF2C-1
67A	BF2C-1	Navy	27	Production variant of XF11C-3/XBF2C-1

Starting with the arbitrarily- designated Model 75 in 1935, Curtiss worked backward to give numerical designations to its earlier models. It skipped a few and ran out of numbers after it reached Model 1, the JN-4 of 1916. Previous models built before the formation of the Curtiss Aeroplane & Motor Company in 1916, were ignored.

U.S. Navy Fighters
of the Second World War
in Action From

squadron/signal publications